Cello Practice, Cello Performance

Cello Practice, Cello Performance

Miranda Wilson

ROWMAN & LITTLEFIELD
Lanham • Boulder • New York • London

Published by Rowman & Littlefield
A wholly owned subsidiary of The Rowman & Littlefield Publishing Group, Inc.
4501 Forbes Boulevard, Suite 200, Lanham, Maryland 20706
www.rowman.com

Unit A, Whitacre Mews, 26-34 Stannary Street, London SE11 4AB

British Library Cataloguing in Publication Information Available

Library of Congress Cataloging-in-Publication Data

Wilson, Miranda.
  Cello practice, cello performance / Miranda Wilson.
      pages cm
  Includes bibliographical references and index.
  ISBN 978-1-4422-4676-8 (hardcover : alk. paper) — ISBN 978-1-4422-4677-5 (pbk. : alk.
paper) — ISBN 978-1-4422-4678-2 (ebook)
  1. Cello—Instruction and study. I. Title.
  MT300.W55 2015
  787.4'193—dc23   2014049732

∞™ The paper used in this publication meets the minimum requirements of
American National Standard for Information Sciences—Permanence of Paper
for Printed Library Materials, ANSI/NISO Z39.48-1992.

Printed in the United States of America

For Gillian Bibby

Contents

Illustrations

FIGURES

TABLES

Acknowledgments

This book would not have been possible without my teachers: Judith Hyatt, Rolf Gjelsten and the other members of the New Zealand String Quartet, Natalia Pavlutskaya, the late Alexander Ivashkin, Phyllis Young, András Fejér and the other members of the Takács Quartet, and Judith Glyde taught me what it meant to be a cellist and inspired me with their artistry.

Neither would it have been possible without my students, who have been a pleasure to teach and who have all had something to teach me: Jordan Asker, Kezia Bauer, Elizabeth Becker, Joshua Bonn, Daniel Ferguson, Chyenne Fisher, Michael Green, Shannon Hall, Stefan Jarocki, Ryan Messling, Micah Millheim, Annabel Ryu, Melissa Searle, Kathryn Smith, Pierce Trey, Kalindi True, and Marilyn Von Seggern tried out dozens of ideas, offered candid feedback, and taught me ideas of their own.

I am grateful to the faculty and staff at the University of Idaho's Lionel Hampton School of Music and Preparatory Division for their practical and collegial support. Special thanks go to the faculty and staff of the University of Idaho Library for their help in tracking down hard-to-find materials.

I owe a particular debt of gratitude to my former colleagues in the Tasman String Quartet, Anna van der Zee, Jennifer Banks, and Christiaan van der Zee, who taught me how to think deeply about sound, intonation, vibrato, theory, and analysis. During the years we worked together, they were my most critical and unrelenting teachers, and I can't thank them enough for the lessons they taught me.

My "cello sisters," Rachel Johnston and Rebecca Turner—brilliant cellists and intuitive teachers—helped me brainstorm many of the ideas in this book.

My family helped me immeasurably during the preparation of this book. Gillian Bibby, Roger Wilson, and Charles Wilson proofread countless drafts, suggesting corrections and clarifications. Corby Butterfield and Mitch Butterfield took care of my household so I had time to write.

Finally, my most heartfelt thanks go to my husband, Sean Butterfield, and our darling daughter, Eliana, for their untiring support, love, and encouragement.

Introduction

The crowded, intensely competitive field of cello playing rates the ability of its performers by a ruthless measure: how they sound on the day of a concert, audition, contest, or exam. It doesn't matter how many hours they've practiced if they can't perform well under pressure. This book demonstrates that effective cello performance, far from being a mysterious gift bestowed upon the lucky few, is a learnable skill that any advanced cellist can acquire through efficient practice.

I wrote *Cello Practice, Cello Performance* because no existing book for advanced cello students and professionals had discussed creative strategies for playing the cello effectively and efficiently at the same time. Many motivational books on effective performing don't account for fundamental problems in instrumental technique that must be fixed before the player can sound good. By the same token, most books on cello playing teach the efficient execution of difficult techniques but seldom discuss how these methods can be the means to an end, that is, an effective performance. This book takes the whole cellist into account, bringing together intellectual and physical aspects of playing the cello from the practice room to the concert hall.

Another problem with existing books on cello playing is that they tend to be divided into sections on left-hand and right-hand techniques, almost as if each hand had little to do with the other.[1] Other artificial distinctions—technique vs. emotion, music theory vs. musical expressiveness, études vs. concert repertoire, solo playing vs. ensemble playing, even "practice-room playing" vs. "performance playing"—can result in inefficient practice habits that lead to ineffective performances.

I propose that the movements of the left and right hands—fingering and bowing—are mutually interdependent, supporting and reinforcing each other in performance. More broadly, "whole-body" cello playing is a holistic theory of efficient musicianship, where musical expression dictates the choice of fingerings and bowings, not the other way around.

This is not a book on cello techniques in the traditional sense. Many authors have already provided exhaustive, and excellent, prescriptions for executing different types of bowstrokes and other techniques. Diran Alexanian's treatise on the subject covered these comprehensively nearly a century ago,[2] and Gerhard Mantel documented the physics and physiology of cello playing in the 1970s.[3] Instead, I assume that the reader has already had the benefit of advanced training in cello fundamentals and repertoire but seeks new ways to improve practice and performance.

Cello Practice, Cello Performance includes dozens of original exercises in whole-body cello playing, demonstrating how efficient intellectual and physical approaches to making music on the cello can rapidly improve the effectiveness of performance. Some of these exercises are unprecedented in the cello literature: one section on efficient breathing while playing the cello adopts techniques from singing, brass pedagogy, and even yoga to eliminate muscular tension and performance anxiety; a detailed discussion of intonation goes through examples from the solo cello and chamber repertoire in all twenty-four major and minor keys to show how different contexts and combinations of instruments call for different approaches to tuning chords.

Other sections address efficient self-teaching methods in the practice room, the creative use of music theory in forming interpretations, the practical applications of scales, the fundamental principles of string-chamber musicianship, and original études that teach how to work on troublesome sections of the major cello repertoire. *Cello Practice, Cello Performance* draws upon the work of practitioners in other fields, from psychology to applied and educational kinesiology, demonstrating techniques to alleviate performance nerves, improve mindfulness and xvi*Introduction*

concentration in the practice room and concert hall, and prevent the interrelated physical and emotional traumas of performance anxiety and repetitive stress injuries.

The art of playing the cello well in performance is an achievable goal. This book provides structured expla- nations of how to get there through mindful listening, movement, and repetition. Based on principles formed during my performing and teaching career, *Cello Practice, Cello Performance* teaches advanced players how to become their own best teachers.

Part I

FUNDAMENTAL PRINCIPLES

Chapter One

Whole-Body Cello Playing

Manus manum lavat. ("One hand washes the other hand.")

As this Roman proverb suggests, when you wash your hands, you can't tell which hand is being washed and which is doing the washing, because both hands are interdependently working at both tasks at the same time. So it should be with the multifaceted, simultaneously performed actions of fingering and bowing on the cello, where both sides of the body must be equally involved in every action.

One of my teachers loved to repeat her credo "Technique is art." The Greek root of the word "technique," she explained, could be loosely translated as "art"; therefore, there was really no distinction between them. I agree wholeheartedly with this belief. In my philosophy of whole-body cello playing, the body and mind work as one.

A central idea of this book is that the musical phrase dictates the way we will use our bodies to create sound from the cello. The whole body—including the mind—is engaged in this pursuit of expressiveness. The breathing of the cellist's lungs is analogous to the breathing motions of the bow arm and the shifting motion of the left arm. All actions are initiated in the torso: by the expansion and contraction of the lungs, the rotational power of the spine, the leading movements of the collarbones, and the distribution of the body's weight in the chair.

If the torso is the center of control, the arms are interdependent workers. The efficient fingering and shifting of the left hand influences and empowers the efficient bowing of the right, and vice versa. Cross-lateral exercises engage both sides of the body and brain—at and away from the cello. All actions are mutually interconnected in the pursuit of cello playing that is both efficient and effective.

In optimal circumstances, efficiency and effectiveness combine inextricably and interdependently to produce nuanced interpretations of music. When technique and art are at one, nothing distracts the audience from their enjoyment of the composer's music and the drama of the performance.

Many cellists, however, play very effectively, but not efficiently. We can see one of the most famous examples of this in Augustus John's portrait of the Portuguese cellist Guilhermina Suggia (1885–1950) that hangs in the Tate Britain gallery in London.[1] Suggia was one of the foremost cellists of her time, though she is more widely known today as the subject of John's painting. Clad in a glamorous red concert gown and posing majestically with her Montagnana cello, Suggia looks like the archetype of the passionate, romantic cellist. Her eyes are closed in concentration, her head turned dramatically to her right, as if following the direction of her fully extended bow arm. We can hear in Suggia's historic recordings that she played the cello effectively,[2] even if some of her stylistic decisions—extreme rubato and frequent glissandi—are no longer fashionable today.

Despite this, as John's portrait and various photographs show quite plainly, Suggia did not play the cello efficiently at all. Her right shoulder was raised, and the tendons of her neck visibly protruded from the tension of her stance and movements. She held the bow tightly, with white knuckles and stiffly straightened fingers. One of Suggia's students, the British cellist Amaryllis Fleming (1925–1999), recalled that Suggia instructed her students to imitate this illogical bow hold, with results that ranged from small tone production to physical injuries.[3] Suggia's genius enabled her to overcome her self-imposed obstacles, but her way of playing didn't appear to work for anyone else.

The opposite of this, efficient playing that is completely deficient in effectiveness, is rarer, since most cellists who are advanced enough to play efficiently also know how to make interpretative decisions. Still, we often describe a musician who plays accurately but without passion as "robotic," and we can find the ultimate example of efficiency without effectiveness in an actual violin-playing robot manufactured by Toyota. This robot, which bears a humorous resemblance to a Stormtrooper, makes perfectly logical, coordinated physical movements, and it can produce a decent sound and tolerable intonation from the instrument. However, its playing has no sense of lyricism in the phrasing or variation in articulations and vibrato.[4]

Cellists may feel relieved that robots cannot yet replace humans in music-making, but many people still lack efficiency in their practice habits. When a cellist is less talented than Guilhermina Suggia—and most of us are—inefficiency breeds ineffectiveness. In common parlance, cellists who play ineffectively are said to have "bad technique." They seem uncoordinated, because the bow can somehow never seem to "catch" the left hand's vibrato, the tone is weak, and the intonation is faulty. When the left hand literally doesn't know what the right hand is doing, this is called *homolaterality*, the opposite of cross-laterality.

A normal, well-coordinated adult body is supposed to function cross-laterally. Homolaterality is normal only in babies who haven't yet learned to crawl. Once babies figure out how to use the arms and legs cross-laterally to move themselves around, all aspects of their development start to progress more rapidly.[5] Cross-laterality helps us walk and perform simple everyday activities and even advanced ones, such as playing the cello; it is what happens when the body is functioning normally. And yet, under conditions of stress, anxiety, and fear, cross-laterality breaks down. Cellists who have mastered the instrument and can play well in a low-stakes setting, such as the practice room, often experience uncontrollable nerves in performance. The heart races, the breathing becomes shallow and irregular, the shoulders lift, the hands shake and sweat, and all the work in the practice room is undone as the cellist misses shifts, veers out of tune, and struggles to express any of the planned nuances of phrasing and articulation. Sometimes, in nightmare situations, the cellist drops the bow or experiences catastrophic memory slips.

This ineffectiveness in performance does not always result from a lack of dedication. Decades after K. Anders Ericsson and his colleagues concluded that 10,000 hours of "deliberate practice" were necessary to acquire expertise in music,[6] we all still know the sad stories of student cellists who practiced with diligence and determination yet never became effective enough players to win a job or make a decent living as a musician.

The main cause of inefficiency and ineffectiveness in cello playing is a lack of coordination between the two sides of the body. But we *can learn* to perform more successfully by using the combined resources of our bodies and minds. The brain–body connection, a well-known aspect of many fields of alternative therapy, has significant practical applications in cello playing. Experts in the fields of applied and educational kinesiology have proposed that performing cross-lateral physical exercises can help us use the two sides of our brain more efficiently. This improves not only our concentration and physical coordination but also our coping strategies for stage fright.

Efficient practice, therefore, must include "both-handed" strategies for accomplishing aspects of playing that learners typically find difficult. The best left-hand movement in the world isn't efficient if the bowstroke doesn't "catch" it, because the motions of the two hands must work as a coordinated whole if the audience is to hear changes in pitch. Similarly, the best *sautillé* bowing will be useless if you only practice it on open strings, because the minute you stop the strings with the fingers of your left hand, you probably won't be able to perform the stroke anymore.

This is why I find it puzzling that so many beginning cello method books start with pages and pages of boring exercises of whole-bow strokes on open strings before the student is allowed to put down fingers on the strings. This is essentially a homolateral method, and it isn't efficient, because any good that the right hand may have accomplished will be forgotten as soon as the student tries to use both hands simultaneously.

Recent studies have shown that the human brain doesn't multitask well,[7] so it makes no sense to try to develop a two-track mind. What would happen if, instead, we treated a traditionally "left-handed" activity such as shifting as a technique that involved the right hand as much as the left? What would happen if we practiced shifts as a whole-body, cross-lateral exercise?

One of the answers, of course, is that we would affect the synaptic connections in our brains. "It's a biological fact that the process of learning any new skill creates physical, structural changes in the brain," writes the neuropsychiatrist Mona Lisa Schulz. "Much research has demonstrated learning-induced changes in the brain. A recent study showed that even learning to juggle objects caused physical changes in brain anatomy."[8] What a liberating thought. If something as relatively easy to learn as juggling can positively affect our brains, it is obvious that we can also affect the brain's plasticity with the "juggling" motions of cross-lateral cello playing, where our arms move in coordinated, interconnected, interdependent ways.

Many cellists and teachers believe that if you don't "have your technique" by the time you reach some milestone age—college age, or even younger—it is too late to enter the music profession seriously. I propose, however, that because our brains are infinitely malleable, it is *always* possible to improve the efficiency and effectiveness of our cello playing.

I developed seven broad principles of cello playing during my years as a student, a young professional in a full-time string quartet, and a professor of cello at the University of Idaho. Together, they form a guide to all the aspects of cello playing in the next chapters:

1. Practice the way you intend to perform, and perform the way you practiced.
2. Listen widely, actively, and analytically to recordings, including recordings of your own playing.
3. Let expressive goals dictate your physical movements at the cello.
4. Let both hands work together on challenging techniques.
5. Analyze closely where and why mistakes happen, and seek both-handed solutions.
6. Practice repetitions of your successes, not of your failures.
7. Breathe.

Chapter Two

Cross-Lateral Warm-Ups for the Fundamentals of Cello Playing

THE STARTING POINT

The goal of whole-body cello playing is to perform effectively, and the exercises in fundamentals shown in this chapter are designed to achieve this goal. The three main facets of effective playing are (a) a resonant tone, (b) clean intonation, and (c) expressive interpretative nuance. These facets are mutually interdependent, since you must simultaneously work on tone and expression when your goal is improved intonation, and so on. Expressiveness is the starting point for all physical aspects of playing the cello; it isn't possible to have one without the other.

WARMING UP

Cellists, like athletes, should warm up before performing, partly to prevent injury and partly to improve performance. One effective way to do this is to practice brain–body connection exercises, both at and away from the cello, that improve the flow of energy between both hemispheres of the brain and both sides of the body.

EVERYDAY EXERCISES FOR PERFORMANCE ENERGY

Anyone who has suffered from performance nerves has—knowingly or otherwise—experienced an impaired flow of energy between their brain and body. The frustrating symptoms of nerves include an elevated heart rate (which can sometimes be so severe that the sufferer imagines he or she is having a heart attack), a dry mouth, shallow breathing, a knot in the stomach, hands that are at once freezing cold and slippery with sweat, tense muscles, and—perhaps the worst of all—the constant babbling interior monologue of self-criticism that threatens to

drown out the music itself. There are many books on the subject of banishing musicians' performance nerves or simply dealing with them so that they're bearable.[1] Most of them recommend practicing certain affirmations to improve self-esteem and confidence. In my experience, however, these practices are beneficial, but they don't entirely solve the physical and psychological problems of learning and performing music.

In my experience as a cellist and teacher, I have found the practices of applied and educational kinesiology to be much more useful in preventing performance nerves and musicians' injuries. These gentle, noninvasive everyday exercises draw on the concept of the human body's energy pathways to improve connections between the brain's hemispheres. I have loosely adapted several exercises from this practice to foster efficient movement and avoid excessive tension in cello playing.

THE CEREBRAL CORTEX

The cerebral cortex is the part of the brain that deals with our senses, our memories, our reasoning, and our decisions. It has two hemispheres, a left hemisphere and a right hemisphere, connected by the corpus callosum. When the brain is functioning optimally, the two halves operate like two powerful computers connected by a cable that enables data to flow in and out of the halves. The right side of the brain controls the left side of the body, and the left side of the brain controls the right side of the body. The function of the left hemisphere is thought to deal with reason and logical thinking; the function of the right is more concerned with emotions and "entire perspective" thinking. Part of what applied and educational kinesiology exercises do is to engage both sides of the brain through physical activity, which improves our concentration and our ability to perform physical tasks.

MALFUNCTIONING UNDER STRESS

When the human body is under stress—particularly the kind of stress that a musician deals with in practice and performance—information doesn't flow so easily across the corpus callosum, and our capacity for logic can be cut off from our capacity for perspective. The left and right sides of the body don't know what the other is doing. Our energy slows down. Our responses slow down. It is almost as if time itself slows down, even though our hearts are pounding and sometimes we even shake with nerves. We become homolateral, which severely obstructs our ability to play the cello in a well-coordinated manner. This is the clumsy, maladroit feeling that is so familiar from stressful situations like auditions, recitals, and examinations. It's also the fuzzy-headed lack of focus that leads us to waste time and accomplish too little in the practice room.

The symptoms of homolaterality happen precisely at the time when we don't want them to, and they are highly distressing. This set of exercises, which I adapted for cellists from the work of several celebrated applied kinesiologists,[2] can improve coordination and concentration when practicing and performing on the cello.

1. CROSS-LATERALITY EXERCISES

Practicing cross-laterality exercises improves our ability to coordinate the left and right sides of our brains and bodies. A good exercise to start with is a cross-lateral march to energize the whole body. The vigor of marching can also help to eradicate feelings of nervousness before a performance. It also works well at the start of a practice session to focus the mind and the breathing.

Cross-Lateral March

1. Remaining in one spot, perform an exaggerated march, raising the right arm at the same time as the left leg (and the left arm at the same time as the right leg). Gradually let your arm movements cross over the middle of your body.
2. Next, while still marching, touch the palms and fingers of your hands to the opposite knees—slap your left knee with your right hand and your right knee with your left hand.
3. After marching for a minute or two, stop. For the sake of comparison, perform a non-cross-lateral march (that is, a homolateral one), where you raise your right arm at the same time as your right leg, and your left arm at the same time as your left leg. Notice how clumsy homolaterality is, compared with the balance

and energy of cross-laterality. If you suddenly feel as if you're about to fall over, this is not unusual—it's the same homolaterality that creates the cellist's terror of dropping the bow on stage or the anxiety-driven inability to coordinate the left-hand fingers with short bowstrokes in fast passages of music, such as Popper's *Elfentanz*.

4. Return to cross-lateral marching. Notice while you're doing it how much easier it is, and how much more naturally you're able to breathe.

When to use the cross-lateral march: when you're having a difficult practice session where you're having trouble shifting or coordinating your arms to play very fast passages. It's also useful for when you can't concentrate. You can even do it discreetly during pauses in orchestral rehearsals, because it works just as well sitting down. Simply put your bow down safely, then raise your right knee and touch it with your left-hand fingers underneath your cello, and your left knee with your right-hand fingers.

Infinity Symbol Exercises

Infinity symbol exercises are a subset of cross-laterality exercises that work extremely well for concentration and energy flow. Resembling a sideways figure eight, the infinity symbol is a mathematical term, but it also has superstitious significance in certain mystical practices, such as *feng shui*. Many children like to doodle infinity symbols on paper—and though they may not realize this, they're practicing an educational kinesiology exercise in hand–eye coordination! These exercises, which I have adapted from Sharon Promislow's *Making the Brain/ Body Connection*,[3] can help cellists use the shape of the infinity symbol to avoid tension, improve bow changes, and distribute weight in a balanced manner while sitting.

Infinity Symbol Exercise 1: Coordinating Eye Movement and Visual Field

1. Breathing deeply in through your mouth and out through your nose, raise one of your arms (it doesn't matter which) and extend it in front of you. Now make an infinity symbol shape in the air, going up in the middle where the lines cross. Keep your head and neck still and relaxed, but follow your hand's movement with your eyes. Notice your breathing; notice how your energy levels change.
2. Now pick up your bow, hold it in your right fist, and point it out ahead of you. Make infinity symbols, following the tip with your eyes. This exercise can help focus your mind and improve your concentration.

3. Take the exercise one step further by picking up your bow in your right hand with a relaxed bow hold as if you're about to play. Holding your bow horizontally in front of you, make infinity symbols in the air. Follow the frog (and your right hand) with your eyes.

Infinity Symbol Exercise 2:
Whole-Body Infinity Symbols

1. Stand with your feet at shoulder-width apart and your arms hanging at your sides. Sway gently from side to side, feeling your weight move from one foot to the other. Let your arms be extremely floppy so that they sway with your body. Feel that your body is moving in the motion of an infinity symbol.

2. Now hold your arms outstretched in front of your body and draw infinity symbols in the air with both arms moving together, going up in the middle where the lines cross. Continue to move your weight from foot to foot, and allow your torso to twist gently as you move your arms. These are movements that you will ultimately use when playing the cello.

3. The next step is to translate these motions into sitting with the cello and the bow. First, holding your cello as you would to play it, practice swaying between your sitz bones[4] until you feel that you're sitting in a balanced manner with your weight equally distributed. You will be swaying from side to side using a slight figure-eight motion: if you find this hard to do, imagine you are looking down at the top of your head as it moves in lateral figure eights. You may find that you illogically but habitually favor weighting one side over the other when you play the cello; this exercise can help to correct the habit. Think of your torso as the "central control unit" in playing the cello. All bowing and shifting motions originate in this part of your body. If your joints are relaxed, there will be no need to think about what the shoulders, elbows, and wrists are doing because they will automatically move efficiently once the back has initiated bowing and shifting, thereby liberating you from the string player's bugbear, the raised right shoulder. Remember that the human spine is by far the strongest part of the body—it holds us up all day so that we can walk around, so it's only logical that it can also power all movements we need for playing the cello.[5]

Infinity Symbol Exercise 3:
Infinity Bowing, Infinity Shifting

1. Pick up your bow. Play any fingered note on the cello (not an open string) using vibrato. Keep your neck relaxed, and think of initiating the bow's motion from the muscles that move the collarbones and the shoulder blades, which, after all, are part of the arms.[6] Sway between your sitz bones in your chair as you bow back and forth, relaxing the heavy weight of your arm into the string. Feel that the side-to-side shifting of your weight in the chair is powering the back-and-forth motion of your bow. As you change bow, make a looping motion in the shape of an infinity symbol in the air with the screw of your bow, as shown in the drawing below (fig. 2.1). (The infinity symbol is lopsided because you need a much bigger loop when changing bow at the tip than you do at the frog.) Because of the curving shape of the bridge, there are several "sides" of each string that you may play on without catching another string. Take care to maintain a consistent contact point between the bow and the string, and check in a mirror that you are always pulling the bow parallel to the bridge—the infinity symbol movement should be done vertically, not laterally. When done correctly, infinity bowing is a much more elegant, less tiring method for changing the bow than a horizontal back-and-forth "sawing" method. The great cellist Leonard Rose is said to have remarked, "There are no straight bows,"[7] and I believe this is what he meant. Infinity bowing, by altering the elevation of the arm over bow changes, not only makes bow changes smoother but also helps create a more resonant tone.

2. Now combine your infinity bowing with infinity shifting. Just as an archer must make a pulling-back motion with the bow and arrow in order to shoot the arrow forward,[8] a cellist must prepare an upwards shift with a pulling-back motion in order to get enough energy to shift quickly and accurately. This kind of shift requires a slight torso rotation to the left to prepare the shift and a slight rotation to the right to execute the shift. Once more, think of the arm's movement originating in the muscles that move the collarbones and shoulder blades. Practice shifting from first position to fourth position on the A-string with your second finger (going from C to F), rotating your torso slightly to initiate your arm's movement. If your elbow could draw a line in the air, it would look like the drawing below (fig. 2.2), starting on the left side. A clockwise pulling-back motion sets the shift into motion, and the arm carries the hand to fourth position.

Figure 2.1.   Infinity bowing

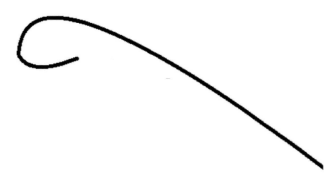

Figure 2.2.   Shifting—upwards trajectory

3. Next, practice shifting backwards from fourth position to first position, from F back to C. The elbow's trajectory does the reverse, as the counterclockwise pulling-back motion activates the shift and carries the hand back to first position. If your elbow could draw a line in the air, it would look like this drawing (fig. 2.3), starting on the right side.

If you practice the exercise shown in figure 2.4, your elbow's path through the air will look something like figure 2.5.

When to use Infinity Symbol Exercises

1. The hand–eye coordination infinity symbol exercises are useful for improving concentration and fine-motor coordination. They are particularly useful as a focusing exercise for people who suffer from attention deficit disorder, as many musicians do.
2. Whole-body infinity symbol exercises are a very relaxing warm-up for practice and a good stress release backstage before a concert. Any side-to-side action

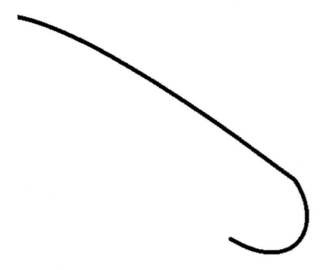

Figure 2.3.   Shifting—backwards trajectory

that crosses over the midpoint of your body, particularly one that also engages the focus of the eyes, helps the hemispheres of your brain communicate better. Such exercises are also very freeing and relaxing for the parts of your body that you use the most in cello playing—back, arms, and hands. It grounds the balance between your feet and between your sitz bones, and it reinforces the idea that all the necessary power in cello playing comes from the torso.

3. Infinity bowing and infinity shifts should become a part of everyday playing. No bowstroke ever needs to be entirely horizontal, and the varied vertical bow angles of infinity bowing can create greater depth and resonance from the string because they "dig into" it better. Getting from note to note always requires forethought and preparation, and infinity shifts are an ideal way to increase shifting accuracy. Even though it may be desirable to practice infinity bowing on long tones without shifting, you should always practice infinity shifts using infinity bowing. To maximize resonance and tone, you should habitually use vibrato in these fundamental exercises as part of your expressive palette of sound colors, varying its speed and amplitude as needed.

2. TAPPING EXERCISES

I have adapted these exercises from the principles of applied kinesiology in Donna Eden's *Energy Medicine* books.[9] Proponents of tapping claim that it can cure a range of physical and psychological ailments, such as addictions and phobias. None of these claims has been scientifically proven,[10] but my students and I have nevertheless found tapping exercises extremely useful in focusing our concentration and banishing feelings of nervousness and anxiety in practice and performances.

1. Place the fingertips of both hands on the soft spot about an inch below your collarbones. These points are known to acupressure practitioners as the K-27 points. Cross your hands over each other—practitioners of applied kinesiology believe this encourages cross-laterality and moves energy between your brain's hemispheres—and, breathing slowly and deeply in through your nose and out through your mouth, firmly tap your K-27 points. Repeat for around thirty seconds.
2. Uncrossing your hands, move your fingertips to the center of your sternum. Using all your fingers and both your thumbs, tap firmly up and down your sternum, continuing to breathe slowly and deeply. Repeat for thirty seconds.

Figure 2.4.   Infinity shift from C to F

3. Now move your hands to the front of your rib cage and, continuing to breathe slowly and deeply, tap this area for thirty seconds.

When to use tapping exercises:

* Backstage before concerts to dispel performance nerves.
* In the practice room when you're having trouble focusing. You can even practice these exercises unobtrusively during breaks in long rehearsals.
* To energize you when you're tired but have to keep working.
* To improve breathing when your lungs feel constricted, either from anxiety or by habitually not breathing well enough.

3. CENTERING EXERCISES

After practicing cross-lateral exercises (including infinity symbol exercises) and tapping exercises, finish your energy warm-up by centering your balance and equilibrium. Sit on the chair you use when you play the cello, with your legs crossed at the ankle and both feet on the floor. Put your palms together in a "praying" position, then move your right hand towards your left shoulder and your left hand towards your right shoulder so that your wrists form an *X* across your chest. (It doesn't matter which wrist is in front.) Keeping your wrists crossed, turn your palms inwards to face your chest, then rotate them further so that you can clasp your hands, interlacing your

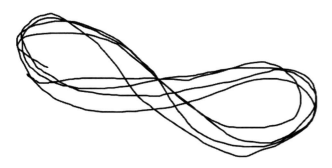

Figure 2.5.   Infinity shifts—back-and-forth trajectory

fingers. Close your eyes and breathe deeply for at least fifteen seconds. Some musicians find it useful to repeat positive affirmations while they practice this exercise.[11] I prefer to listen to my breath and enjoy the feeling of calm and concentration.

4. BREATHING AND PLAYING

String players usually breathe inefficiently and shallowly while making music, and this tendency is exacerbated under stressful conditions, such as performance. The tendency to hold the breath for long periods and then to emit distractingly audible gasps and sniffs is near-universal; we can hear it in the recordings of even the greatest cellists, such as Pablo Casals. Cellists tend to inhale sharply and audibly through their noses before beginning the first note of a piece or when cueing other players, and under the stress of performing, the ragged exhalation that follows can contribute to the cellist's worst enemy, the uncontrollably shaking or bouncing bow.

Deep breathing is often recommended as an aid to expressiveness[12] and an antidote to performance anxiety; however, if you aren't accustomed to breathing efficiently, it's a little late to try to cultivate the skill in the greenroom ten minutes before the concert. What's more, nerves can sometimes be so strong that we feel unable to draw deep breaths of air into our lungs. Because of this, I recommend practicing tapping exercises before breathing ones to help relax the rib cage. Once you are relaxed enough to breathe deeply, practice the following exercises.

Basic calming breathing: Breathe in through your mouth and out through your nose. This method is in direct opposition to the breathing advice of many alternative therapy practitioners, who recommend breathing in through the nose and out through the mouth. I find it more useful to imitate breathing exercises from brass pedagogy, where the quality of breathing is cardinal to the quality of sound.[13] Breathing in through your nose can cause tension in the nose, throat, and lungs; breathing in through your mouth enables you to expand your lungs with less resistance. Breathing out slowly through the nose provides a little resistance; this will help you "breathe through" the resistance of your bow's hair against your string when you play. When you inhale, you should sense movement as your chest expands, but without intentionally moving any part of your body. Some people let their shoulders rise when they breathe, but this contributes to tension and should be avoided.[14]

Alternate-nostril breathing: This yoga technique is another calming exercise. Block off your left nostril with your left thumb and inhale through your right nostril. Then block your right nostril with your right ring finger and exhale through your left nostril. Repeat for fifteen seconds.[15]

Bowing and breathing: Practice the exercise below (fig. 2.6) to improve your breathing while playing and, by extension, to improve your sound. Like the first breathing exercise, it works best with mouth inhalation and nose exhalation. You may play this exercise on any stopped note you wish, but don't use an open string—all techniques work best when approached with both hands. Because this exercise is derived from yoga, I usually use the second finger, which has special significance in certain yogic breathing and meditation exercises. Use a continuous vibrato for optimal tone quality. Notice in exercises (a) and (b) how strongly we inadvertently associate the down-bow with the out-breath and the up-bow with the in-breath. Exercise (a) makes the traditional bowing–breathing association, but exercise (b) turns this assumption on its head. Notice the feeling of exhaling on an up-bow, which may be unfamiliar. Exercises (c) and (d) remove the association of the changing bow and the changing breath. Notice how it feels to change breath in the middle of the bow, instead of at the frog or at the tip. You can practice this exercise doing slow scales or single notes. You will hear an immediate improvement in your sound, because deliberate breathing has the pleasant by-product of relaxing the muscles cellists typically tense: trapezius, deltoids, and biceps. This will enable the arm's weight to relax efficiently into the string.

You may feel a little light-headed when you first practice this exercise. This is normal and simply means that you aren't used to breathing deeply. But practice it for a short time at first, and then gradually work up to longer periods as your breathing habits improve.

Next, practice breathing "through" shifts, continuing to breathe in through the mouth and out through the nose. One of the main reasons cellists miss big shifts in performance—regardless of how well they went in the practice room—is the widespread tendency to hold the breath before executing a difficult technique, such as

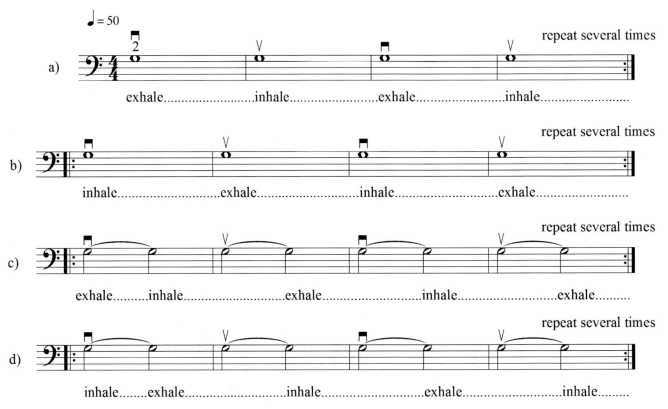

Figure 2.6.   Breathing through the bow on a single note

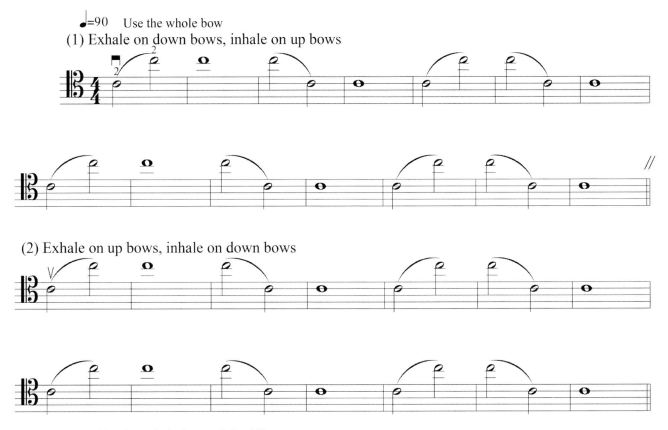

Figure 2.7.   Breathing through the bow and the shift

shifting. This causes the rest of the upper body to tense up and move inefficiently. The following exercise (fig. 2.7) is an experiment in the different combinations of down-bow vs. up-bow, shifting up vs. shifting down, and inhaling vs. exhaling. Use a healthy tone, whole bows, and a continuous vibrato as you practice it. Feel how the power of breathing helps both tone production and left-hand accuracy in shifts.

Every time you practice, whether you're playing an exercise, a scale, an étude, or repertoire, start to pay conscious, deliberate attention to your breathing. If at first you have trouble observing how you breathe, ask another person to hold the chest-piece of a stethoscope against your chest or back while you play and listen to your breathing. Listen to recordings of your practice sessions and performances, noting where you have a tendency to breathe, gasp, or sniff audibly. Because mouth breathing can look distracting, it isn't practical to breathe in through your mouth in performance, so gradually replace mouth inhalation with nose inhalation in your practice, taking care to keep all breaths relaxed and quiet. Paying attention to breath while playing is a learned skill that takes a great deal of mindfulness and concentration, but after a while it will become natural and even easy.

Chapter Three

The Inherent Expressiveness of Good Intonation

THE ILLUSION OF OBJECTIVITY IN INTONATION[1]

Intonation is part of tone, and yet it is also one of the most misunderstood aspects of musicianship. Many cellists play out of tune or only approximately in tune, but they don't realize it or don't know how to fix the problem. Some think a perfectly tuned piano is an objective source of intonation, and they try to play every note of a piece against the piano's equivalent pitches. This doesn't work very well for the resonance of the cello, however, because the equal-tempered system of piano tuning is itself a compromise, invented so that pianists could play approximately in tune in any key. The only reason we think the piano's equal-tempered triads are in tune is because we are used to the way they sound.

Some musicians believe that the digital tuner is the answer to all intonation problems, assuming that if they can learn to play every pitch of a composition in tune with a tuner, they will have perfect intonation. This doesn't work either. Leaving aside for now the fact that "tuner tuning" is not necessarily the best guide for cello intonation, tuners will register expressive nuances, such as vibrato, dynamic changes, and certain bow attacks, as alterations of the pitch. What's more, playing into a tuner isn't a good way to train the ear. Even if a cellist could play every single note into a tuner with perfect results, this progress would vanish once the tuner was turned off, because truly internalized tuning must be done with the ears, not the eyes. The tuner, in other words, is only useful for tuning the open strings of the cello, not for anything else.

In reality, there is no perfect system for playing objectively in tune on the cello. Every possibility for intonation is a compromise of some kind, but we can search for the best solutions. The best guideline for intonation on the cello is not to tune individual pitches, but to cultivate a fine sense of relative pitch that enables us to tune notes within the context of melody, harmony, and the resonances of the four open strings.

TOOLS FOR INTONATION

Many musicians share an axiomatic idea that string instruments are the only instruments aside from the human voice that can be perfectly in tune. This is not completely true. Intonation on a string instrument is markedly different from intonation in human voices because even though the left-hand fingers have the capacity to alter pitches infinitesimally, the cellist still has to work within a system of four open strings to obtain the best resonance.[2] When we play a fingered D, for example, the physical makeup of the cello demands that we use the open D-string as a reference pitch, because a fingered D that is perfectly in tune with the open D-string will cause the open string to resonate sympathetically. Finding this resonance is an important part of being able to produce a good tone. Notes that do not correspond with the open strings should be pitched according to their relation to open strings: for example, we can find E-flat by relating it to the open G-string. This method is principally useful for solo cello playing or chamber music that involves only string instruments. When playing with the piano, however, we must find a way to combine the cello's intonation system with the piano's system. There are still more systems for playing with other wind instruments and with large ensembles, such as chamber and symphony orchestras.

THE MARRIAGE OF MUSIC THEORY AND INTONATION: NEGOTIABLE AND NON-NEGOTIABLE INTERVALS

Melody and harmony are the starting points for intonation on the cello. This is because Western music written between approximately 1600 and approximately 1900—that is, the period a large proportion of the cello's repertoire comes from—uses various forms of functional diatonic harmony. Intervallic relations between notes—whether they sit side by side, as in melody, or sound together, as in harmony—are key factors in intonation. There are certain intervals whose intonation is "negotiable" and others whose intonation is "non-negotiable." The non-negotiable ones are the perfect consonances: unisons, perfect fourths, perfect fifths, and octaves, which must be played perfectly in tune to avoid an unpleasant, grating tone.

The tuning of all the other intervals—minor and major seconds, minor and major thirds, tritones, minor and major sixths, minor and major sevenths—can vary greatly, depending on the context. When tuning major and minor triads, in most circumstances the root of the chord must be tuned according to a reference pitch, such as an open string. The fifth of the chord must be perfectly tuned to the root. The third, however, is open to negotiation. In string chamber music, players will often tune the third of a major triad slightly flat and the third of a minor triad slightly sharp. How much this is done will depend on many factors, such as the timbre of the group's sound, the dynamics, the type of attack used, and so on.

Because of the predominance of triadic harmony in the cello's repertoire, the detailed study of the materials of music—theory, analysis, counterpoint, aural skills, orchestration—is essential. When preparing a piece of solo or chamber music, cellists should go through the full score with a pencil, writing Roman numeral analyses of chord, in order to determine which voice of the chord the cello and other instruments are playing. This will help in deciding how best to tune the note.

LINEAR INTONATION VS. HARMONIC INTONATION: PLAYING HORIZONTALLY AND VERTICALLY

The kind of intonation a cellist uses in a solo piece is markedly different from the kind that is necessary when playing with a pianist or in an orchestra. The intonation a cellist will use when playing the melody in a string quar-

tet will also be different from the intonation when playing the supporting harmony.

WHAT IS LINEAR INTONATION?

Pablo Casals pioneered a technique he called "expressive intonation,"[3] which works well in a linear (that is, melodic) context (fig. 3.1). This flexible system distinguishes between diatonic and chromatic half-steps in melody: Casals believed that although the tonic, fourth, and fifth degrees of the major scale must be played as strict perfect consonances against each other, the third degree of the scale is "attracted" to the fourth, as is the leading tone to the tonic. In this system, the third degree and leading tone are therefore played slightly sharp. Because of this, the other tones of the scale must adjust: the second and sixth degrees must also be sharpened. (In minor keys, the third is "attracted" to the second degree and is therefore played slightly flatter.)

This system works quite well for playing melodic lines. However, when playing double-stops and chords in solo works such as Bach's cello suites (BWV 1007–1012), or when the cello plays a voice of a chord in an ensemble such as a string quartet, the raised-third/raised-seventh system can sound out of tune. This is where a vertical (i.e., harmonic) approach to intonation works better.

WHAT IS HARMONIC INTONATION?

My system of harmonic intonation is an adaptation of the concept of just intonation.[4] Harmonic intonation on the cello is structured around the resonance of the instrument's open strings. Harmonic intonation is a little more complicated than linear intonation. It is definitely possible to teach oneself the principles of harmonic intonation on solo cello, but I feel that the easiest way to understand and internalize it is with a small string chamber ensemble, such as a string trio, a string quartet, or even a cello trio or quartet. Playing in ensembles is an essential part of a cellist's education, not least because learning to blend sounds with other string players involves thoughtful, experimental work in tuning chords.

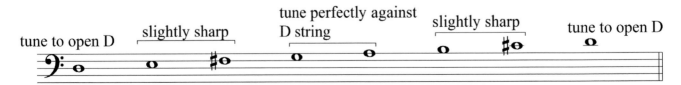

Figure 3.1.   D major scale using Casalsian linear intonation

STEP-BY-STEP HARMONIC INTONATION: TUNING TRIADS AND SEVENTH CHORDS

1. The first step is to make sure the cello and other instruments are tuned correctly. If you tune all the strings of the cello in perfect fifths with each other, it's obvious that the C-string will be out of tune with the A-string. (Incidentally, it will also be out of tune with the piano, which is why you should tune your C-string, not just your A-string, with the corresponding piano key when playing cello-piano pieces.) It's therefore necessary to tune the C-string fractionally sharp. Set a digital tuner or tuning application[5] to 440, and tune your A-, D-, and G-strings. Now set the tuner to 441 and tune the C-string. The pitches of your strings will be A = 220 Hz, D = 146.8 Hz, G = 98 Hz, and C = 65.6 Hz.

2. If playing with a viola, have the player tune the viola strings the same way as you have tuned the cello strings—an octave higher, of course.

3. If playing with violins, have the players tune the A-, D-, and G-strings exactly with the cello strings, then test the violins' E-strings against the viola and cello C-strings. Tune the violins' E-strings as flat as bearably possible so that it sounds passably in tune with the viola and cello C-string. You may even need to adjust the viola and cello C-strings up a little. (Many professional quartets use a different system, in which the cellist tunes the A-string to the 442 setting on the

tuner, the D-string and G-string to the 443 setting, and the C-string to the 444 setting. This removes the necessity for tuning the violin E-string down, but it sacrifices the perfection of the tuning of the fifth between the A- and D-strings, which some players find difficult to deal with. This system is only recommended for when an ensemble has already practiced harmonic intonation intensively.)

4. Now play a major triad with your ensemble. Depending on the number and type of instrumentalists you have, you may not be able to play it as it appears below (fig. 3.2); in this case, simply revoice the chord depending on the available instrumentalists. The cellist should start on D, using a fingered note and not the open string. Use very slow, full bowstrokes and a contact point close to the bridge to create a strong "core" sound. The contact point is very important here, because it is much easier to blend with, and play "against," the overtones of a well-projected tone. Avoid making a wishy-washy tone near or over the fingerboard, because it makes group intonation difficult. (As a side note, it is best to avoid vibrato in the first stages of group tuning. Add it in later when the group has learned the basics of harmonic intonation together, making sure the players agree upon vibrato amplitude and speed, since a wildly different vibrato can stick out of the texture and make chords sound out of tune.)

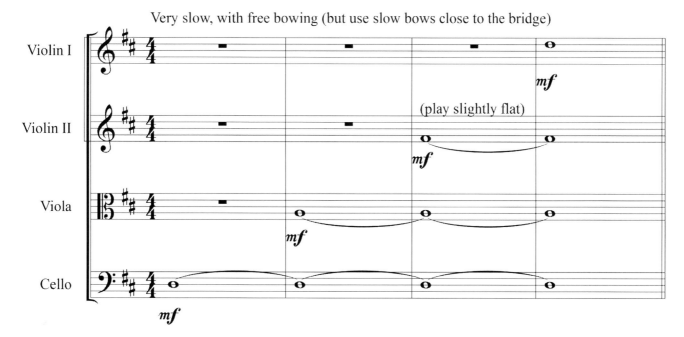

Figure 3.2.   Tuning a D major triad

5. Next, the viola enters with the fifth of the chord, tuning it perfectly against the root. The violist should match the slow bow speed and close-to-bridge contact point of the cellist. A matching tone is vital to good intonation in the group sound. This may be difficult at first, but it gets much easier with time, as witnessed by the characteristic blended tone quality of high-profile chamber ensembles and orchestras. (Building a group sound takes time and patience, which is why casually formed "gigging" groups with high personnel turnover rates usually don't sound as good as full-time, same-personnel ensembles, even when the individual instrumentalists are accomplished players.)

6. Now one of the violins enters with the third, matching the bow speed and contact point of the cellist and violist. As opposed to the sharpened third of Casalsian linear intonation, the third in harmonic intonation should be slightly *flat*. You will have to play around with this, adjusting as necessary, experimenting with different degrees of flatness until—sometimes with a little "aha!" of recognition—you realize you're playing a perfectly tuned triad. You will know when this happens because the resonance of the group sound will improve.

7. Lastly, the violin doubling the root of the chord enters.

8. Now alter the chord so that it has a seventh, forming a D^7 chord (fig. 3.3). In harmonic intonation, the player who has the seventh should pitch it somewhat lower than it would sound in linear intonation. One of the reasons a flatter seventh degree sounds better in harmonic intonation is because the chord resonates better on the instruments. Another relates to voice-leading in the rules of Mozartean harmony (i.e., the kind in harmony textbooks), where the voice that plays the seventh degree of a V^7 chord always resolves downwards to become the third in the chord of resolution.

9. Next, tune a minor triad (fig. 3.4). The third degree in a major triad should be played rather flat; the third in a minor triad should be slightly sharpened.

WHEN TO USE LINEAR INTONATION

Linear intonation works best in a melodic context, that is, when the cello has a solo melodic line. The prime example of this is when playing scales. The Casalsian model of the raised third and seventh degrees works well in major scales. Many inexperienced players struggle with intonation in scales and find themselves migrating sharp on the way up and flat on the way down—sometimes to the extent that they inadvertently end up playing an entire half-step out of tune, particularly in higher positions. This happens because their ears haven't yet learned to hear relative pitch well. Anyone can train his or her ear to listen more acutely, however. One of the best ways to develop this ability is to study sight-singing using *solfège*, which is essentially a way to internalize and verbalize music theory. Another is to play with a recorded drone that corresponds with the tonic note and then tune all other notes against it. It very quickly becomes easier to hear where the pitches should lie without the aid of the drone.

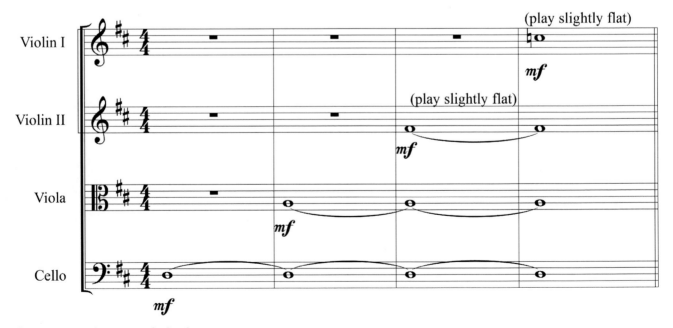

Figure 3.3.   Tuning a seventh chord

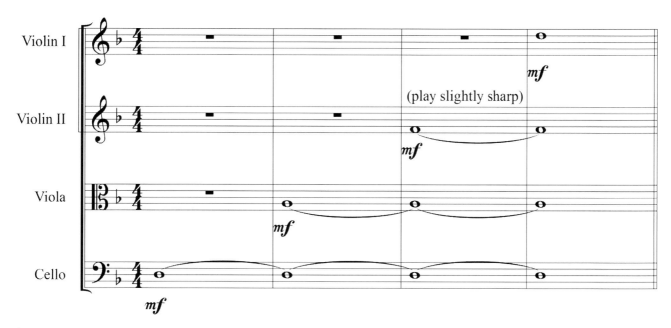

Figure 3.4.   Tuning a D minor triad

Linear intonation also works well in cello-piano compositions. The exception to this is when the cello must play in unison with the piano. In this case, there is no choice but to tune exactly to the piano. Therefore, in the first movement of Beethoven's Cello Sonata op. 69, the tuning of the first theme is different depending on the context. At the opening, the cello is unaccompanied and therefore free to tune linearly (fig. 3.5). Suggested sharpened notes are marked with an *S*: the primary examples are the third (C-sharp) and the seventh (G-sharp), but also the notes that correspond with them at perfect intervals (such as the F-sharp, which must be perfectly in tune with the C-sharp). This same linear intonation will also work at the beginning of the recapitulation, where the piano harmonies do not directly conflict with the cello's solo line (fig. 3.6).

Close to the end of the movement, however, when the piano and cello declaim this theme in emphatic unison, the cellist has no choice but to tune perfectly to the intonation of the piano (fig. 3.7). Because the piano's more percussive attack tends to dominate the texture in this instrumental combination, the cello will not sound "out of tune with itself" when the cellist plays perfectly in tune with the piano.

WHEN TO USE HARMONIC INTONATION

Harmonic intonation works best when the cello is playing in a chordal context. This may be in the context of a chamber work, or in double-, triple-, and quadruple-stops in solo playing. Scales in thirds and sixths should be part of a daily practice routine because this is the best way to incorporate harmonic intonation into everyday warm-ups.

In this major scale in thirds, suggested intonation is written in two lines of text above the staff (fig. 3.8). The upper line corresponds to the upper note, and the lower line corresponds to the lower note. "Fl." indicates a note that should be played slightly flat, "SR" indicates a note that should be perfectly in tune with the corresponding open string in order to take advantage of the sympathetic resonance, and "Open" indicates an open string. (The "SR" above the E on the penultimate third indicates that this E should be played in tune with the A-string. Fingered E that is perfectly in tune with the A-string causes the string to vibrate sympathetically—not as much as a perfectly tuned fingered A does, but enough to be noticeable. Note also that there are two possible ways of tuning an E in this scale: the second chord specifies a flat E against the G that corresponds to open G. Where there is no clear answer to an intonation problem, experimentation will be necessary.)

One feature of this type of tuning is that all major thirds are tuned narrowly and all minor thirds are tuned widely. Student players may have trouble understanding the patterns of major and minor thirds that occur in the major scale, and they may be confused that major thirds are played with a "normal" hand position, whereas minor thirds are played in extended position. Players should memorize the "M3-m3-m3-M3-M3-m3-m3-M3" pattern.

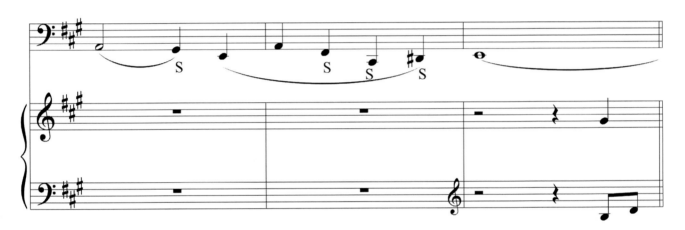

Figure 3.5.   Ludwig van Beethoven, Cello Sonata in A Major, op. 69, movt. I, mm. 1–6

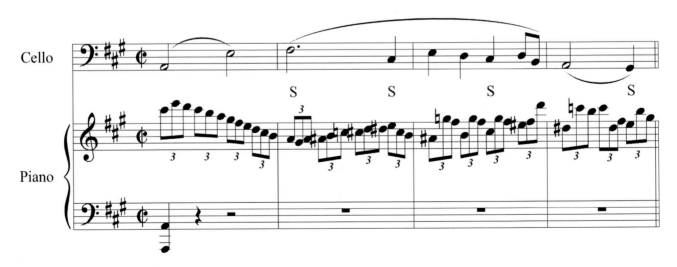

Figure 3.6.   Ludwig van Beethoven, Cello Sonata in A Major, op. 69, movt. I, mm. 152–55

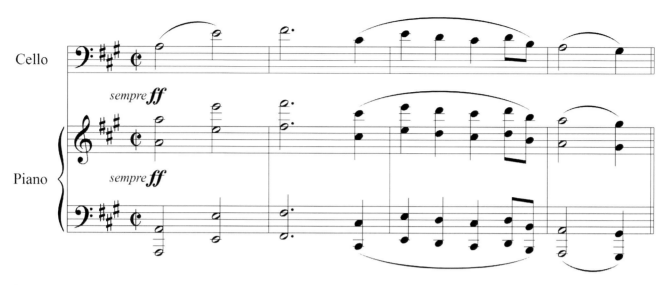

Figure 3.7.   Ludwig van Beethoven, Cello Sonata in A Major, op. 69, movt. I, mm. 253–56

Figure 3.8.   Harmonic intonation of a D major scale in thirds

Tips for tuning scales in thirds: pick one note of the double-stop to tune the other to—don't try to adjust both notes of an out-of-tune third at once. In D major (or another scale with several notes corresponding to open strings), the note you tune to should be the note that corresponds to an open string, and it should be tuned exactly in tune with that string. The other note should be adjusted to this note using harmonic intonation. In a scale that has far fewer notes that correspond to open strings, such as A-flat minor, you will need a different system. The starting point should be figuring out where you are going to place the A-flat. This will directly affect where you place the D-flat and E-flat. The other notes are more "subjective," but the general guideline of "major thirds narrow, minor thirds wide" still applies. If unsure, tuning the entire scale against an A-flat drone (set at the desired frequency) will help.

Harmonic intonation is also applicable to scales in sixths. Because the interval of a sixth is a third inverted, the rules of tuning are the same: a major sixth should be tuned narrowly (because a minor third is tuned widely) and a minor sixth is tuned widely (because a major third is tuned narrowly). Again, players should memorize the pattern of major and minor sixths: "m6-M6-M6-m6-m6-M6-M6-m6."

Tips for tuning scales in sixths: some players will be confused by the concept of major and minor sixths, because their ears may be drawn to the upper note. This causes them to misidentify major sixths as minor, and minor sixths as major. A more beneficial strategy may be to memorize the intervals types in relation to fingering patterns. For example, note that the minor sixth is played using adjacent fingers, whereas the major sixth usually uses 1 and 3 or 2 and 4 in the neck position. When it comes to intonation, tune minor sixths more widely than in equal temperament, and major sixths more narrowly (fig. 3.9).

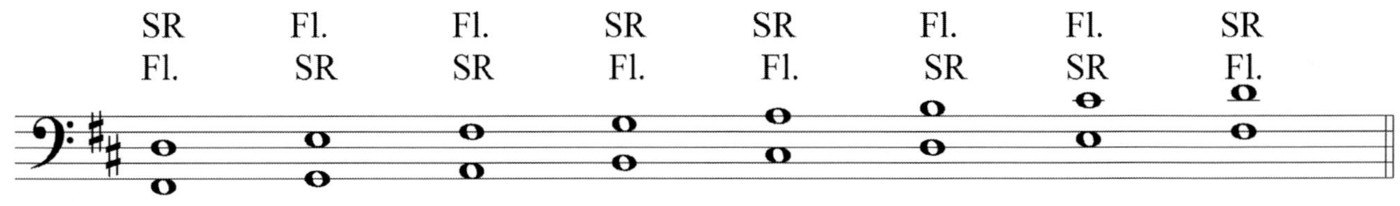

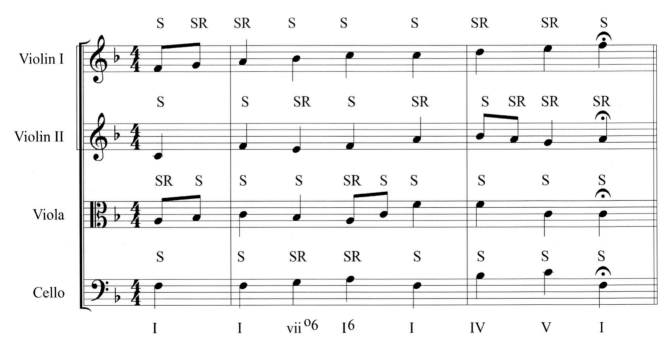

Figure 3.9.   Harmonic intonation of a D major scale in sixths

The only scale in double-stops that does not use harmonic intonation is the scale in octaves. This should be played using linear intonation because its conception is melodic rather than chordal. A tip for improving intonation in octave scales is to focus your concentration more on the lower note than the upper note. Because the ear is naturally drawn to the higher-pitched note, it makes sense to pay greater attention to the lower-pitched one. If you practice listening more closely to the lower note and then adjust the upper note to it, your upper notes will eventually start falling into place more naturally and easily.

Ensemble music usually demands the use of harmonic intonation. Some of the best exercises for learning and improving harmonic intonation are J. S. Bach's four-part chorales. These can be easily played by a number of different instrumental combinations, from a four-cello ensemble to a string quartet to a violin-viola-cello-bass quartet. It is a good idea to go through them making a Roman numeral analysis to determine the chord types

and voicings. Then write in "S," "Fl.," and so on, and experiment with tuning.

This arrangement of Bach's chorale "Solang ein Gott im Himmel lebt" from the church cantata *O Ewigkeit, du Donnerwort*, BWV 20, is an excellent exercise in tuning chords in the key of F major (fig. 3.10). Since we will take an "A-string F"—that is, an F tuned against the open A-string and thus slightly sharp—we will also pitch the B-flats and Cs slightly sharp. (C will be slightly sharper than the cello and viola open C-strings, which should be tuned as sharp as is bearable.) Gs, As, Ds, and Es will be tuned exactly to the open strings for sympathetic resonance. As always, intonation should come from the root of the chord. Identify the root, which is often, but not always, played by the cello, and build the chord from it. Check the root of the chord against the fifth to make sure it is absolutely pure; then add the third, then the seventh if applicable. Listen constantly to make sure the sound has a consistent core and projecting overtones.

Figure 3.10.   Johann Sebastian Bach, "Solang ein Gott im Himmel lebt" from *O Ewigkeit, du Donnerwort*, BWV 20, mm. 1–2 (arranged for string quartet by Miranda Wilson)

ARPEGGIOS

The one type of monophony that should be played with harmonic intonation is arpeggios (fig. 3.11). Although they are linear in composition, arpeggios are a good way to practice harmonies, since they appear in music as a harmonic accompaniment to a melody. This arpeggio exercise, which covers inversions of various chords, is a study in linearly played harmonic intonation. Use a drone and a metronome to practice arpeggios in a variety of tempi; this is the most useful method for training your ear for intonation and your arm in infinity shifting (see chapter 2) at the same time.

WHEN TO USE MORE THAN ONE SYSTEM OF INTONATION

There will be occasions when both linear and harmonic intonation systems are called for within a single movement or even within a single phrase, depending on context. When the phrase is linearly composed, linear intonation should be the player's intuitive response. When there are chords, harmonic intonation usually works best. Bach's cello suites, in particular, require us to switch seamlessly between intonation systems. The Prelude from Cello Suite no. 2 in D Minor, BWV 1008, for example, is chiefly linear, so in the first few measures,

Figure 3.11.   Harmonic intonation in arpeggios

Figure 3.12.   Johann Sebastian Bach, Cello Suite no. 2 in D Minor, BWV 1008, Prelude, mm. 1–4

the third degree of the D minor scale (that is, F) will be pitched slightly flat, and so will the sixth degree, B-flat. The leading tone (C-sharp) will be sharp (fig. 3.12).

But although the first Menuet from the same suite begins with the same set of pitches as the Prelude—a D minor triad—the nonlinear presentation of those pitches indicates that we should use harmonic intonation in the first two measures (fig. 3.13). The first chord, a D minor triad, demands a slightly sharp F, and the chord in the

second measure, an incomplete V^7/III, needs both third and seventh degrees to be slightly flat in order to sound in tune.

The Allemande requires the cellist to switch from using harmonic intonation to linear within the first measure in such a way that there are two differently tuned Fs (fig. 3.14). Although this may feel counterintuitive, the results will not sound jarring because both the chord and the linear passage will be appropriately tuned.

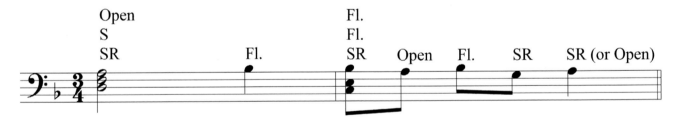

Figure 3.13.   Johann Sebastian Bach, Cello Suite no. 2 in D Minor, BWV 1008, Menuet I, mm. 1–2

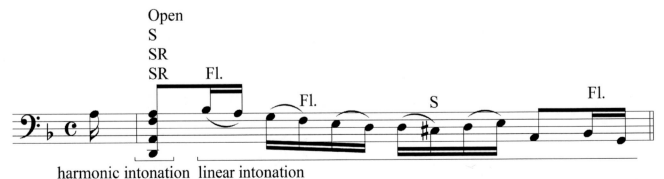

Figure 3.14.   Johann Sebastian Bach, Cello Suite no. 2 in D Minor, BWV 1008, Allemande, mm. 1–2

SUMMARY OF INTONATION GUIDELINES

- Finding good intonation on the cello is a matter of combining certain reference pitches (open strings, piano accompaniment) with the expressive possibilities of relative pitch.
- Non-negotiable intervals (perfect intervals) are played with the same tuning regardless of whether their presentation is melodic (linear) or harmonic (chordal).
- Negotiable intervals (all other intervals) may be played with different tunings depending on context. For example, in the linear intonation system pioneered by Casals, a melodically played major third will be somewhat wide. In harmonic intonation, however, the interval of a major third sounds good when played somewhat narrowly.
- When practicing tuning in a group, remember that the group sound will affect how intonation works. Remember always to practice intonation with a core to the sound. Don't make the mistake of playing very quietly over the fingerboard with minimal arm weight because you're "listening." It is much easier to hear group intonation when the contact point is closer to the bridge and the bow is pulled slowly. This type of tone doesn't necessarily have a loud dynamic, but its overtones make it easier to listen and respond to.
- In all cases, experimentation and discussion is the key to good intonation. Intonation is an inexact science and incompatible with a doctrinaire attitude. The way we tune a triad or a seventh chord will vary depending on many factors: instrumentation, timbre, texture, dynamics, register, attack, and so forth. Keep an open mind and try the ideas and suggestions of mentors and colleagues.

Chapter Four

Solutions to the Challenges of Cello Playing

The fundamental challenges of good cello playing are those same characteristics that epitomize the cello in the popular imagination. Take the most beloved cello piece of all, "The Swan" from *Carnival of the Animals*, by Camille Saint-Saëns. When played well, it showcases the celebrated expressive qualities of cello playing: a resonant, projecting, many-shaded tone, and long, singing phrases where each note moves gracefully to the next. When played poorly, it shows up all kinds of distracting physical habits that detract from the beauty of Saint-Saëns's melodic line: an unevenly pulled bow, a weak attack, an inconsistent vibrato, inept shifts, and so on.

Every one of these problems has a cross-lateral, whole-body solution. This is not a cello technique book in the traditional sense, with pages of photographs showing "correct" and "incorrect" positions for bowing and fingering,[1] but I offer these solutions on the presumption that a certain standard of fundamental efficiency has been mastered. Human bodies vary hugely, so there can be no single correct method for holding the cello and bow, but it is only logical to play with both hands in a relaxed, rounded shape. The thumbs should oppose the middle fingers, both on the stick of the bow and the neck of the cello. The fingers of both hands should, in most circumstances, keep their natural spacing—after all, the cello and bow were designed with the human hand in mind!—and not wedged together as in a salute, or forced widely apart in a tense grasp. Lastly, both hands should pronate slightly, that is, turn inwards to enable an efficient bow-pull in the right, and ease of moving between pitches in the left.

CHALLENGE NO. 1: TONE, RESONANCE, AND PROJECTION

How it should sound

The ideal tone is one that resonates and projects to the back of a performance space, regardless of the dynamics or the mood of the music. Under the right conditions, even a hushed *pianissimo* can be audible in the back row of a large auditorium. The cellist should be able to sustain this tone consistently.

What often happens

The problem is that few of us can practice in a concert hall every day, so we often have to make do with small practice spaces. A tone that sounds perfectly big and attractive under your ear in your living room or a college practice room may not sound this way at all in a larger space. It can be shocking to realize that your tone is small and uneven in a concert hall and that it has no hope of projecting above even the most discreet of pianists.

Myths about tone

Some conductors, trying to inject some energy into lackluster string sections, shout, "More bow, strings!" By this, they mean a faster bow speed that covers more of the length of the bow hair. But "more bow" in itself doesn't improve tone. "More bow" is a means to an end—a bigger tone—but because it isn't the goal in itself, it can't be what governs sound production. Asking for more bow just encourages players to saw back and forth on the surface of the string without necessarily improving resonance or projection. If you use more bow without adjusting any other aspect of bow technique, the result is an unfocused, "skating," uninteresting tone. Trying to isolate a single aspect of string technique, such as "more bow," throws an entire system out of balance as all other aspects struggle to accommodate it. (Similarly, "less bow" is not necessarily an efficient method for playing in quiet dynamics.)

Solutions

The way to approach the problem of a weak tone should be related to the end goal: does it sound good right now, and if not, why not? To fix a sound problem, you can adjust individual components of the system, but you have to account for the fact that other components will be affected and changed. The philosophy of whole-body cello playing is results-based; therefore, the catchphrase should be "More *sound*, strings!"

The chief components of a good tone are summed up by what I call the "Tone Triangle." These three interreliant qualities are (a) contact point, (b) arm weight, and (c) bow speed. The cellist must support and reinforce this Tone Triangle with clean intonation and consistent vibrato in the left hand, because without these the resonance and projection of the tone will be much smaller.

1. The contact point where the bow meets the string should, under most circumstances, be relatively close to the bridge. Bowing on this part of the string provides the optimal conditions for projection, regardless of dynamics. This is a paradigm shift for many players who are accustomed to practice-room acoustics, where not much projection is called for. It isn't possible to play close to the bridge all the time—sometimes the required bowstroke would make it impossible to hear a core in the fundamental pitch of the note clearly—but in general, most cellists greatly improve their tone by moving the bow slightly closer to the bridge.

2. Arm weight is the component of tone that is sometimes called "bow pressure." The words we use in cello-playing discourse can be powerfully physically suggestive, and for this reason "pressure" isn't a good word. It implies a downward push, a tight claw of a bow hand, and a tense, raised right shoulder. It is much better to imagine channeling the heavy weight of the human arm into the string and "pulling through" the string using the initiating movements of the collarbones and the gentle rotational power of the spine. Contrary to the common practice of gripping the bow firmly, the right hand should hold it as lightly as possible—so lightly that if it were any lighter, the bow might fall to the floor. The concept of applying more arm weight to bowing is significantly easier if the player makes the lower half of the bow—from the frog to a couple of inches beyond the balance point—the "default setting" in which to do most of the bowing, and to which to return after an excursion to the upper half. The frog is, after all, the strongest, heaviest part of the bow.

3. The speed of the bow will usually need to be rather slow when the contact point is very close to the bridge and the arm weight is particularly heavy. (Indeed, one of the top problems in preprofessional cello playing happens when players simply pull the bow too fast and too far from the bridge. This produces a small, nonresonant, nonprojecting tone.) The bow-pull should always be as close to parallel with the bridge as you can get it, taking into account the "infinity symbol" (see chapter 2) shape of the bow changes. A too-fast speed will produce a sound with no core that only has the ghostly noise of the overtones. The benefits of a slowish bow speed include not running out of bow in a slow piece like "The Swan," where legato phrasing is ultra-important.

The exception to the general rule of playing close to the bridge is for short bowstrokes, such as staccato and controlled spiccato. Short strokes need to project a pitch and a tone color, and it is not always possible to do this when playing very close to the bridge.

How to practice making a projecting tone using the Tone Triangle

When making adjustments to any of the three components, be sure to play with a stopped, vibrated note, not an open string. This is because making improvements to any technique should be a both-handed activity. If intonation is poor, the tone will be poor: left-hand actions are as inextricable a component of tone as right-hand actions, because tone, intonation, and vibrato are all integrated parts of our sound.

Also remember that Tone Triangle playing won't necessarily sound good in your practice space. The goal is to practice what will sound good in a concert space. With this in mind, don't be afraid of a small amount of harshness or scratching under your ear. Some slight harshness will probably not project as far as the audience as long as the fundamental pitch of a note—the core of the sound—has a focused and resonant tone. Whenever possible, practice in a large space with a knowledgeable colleague sitting far away from you and listening out for what projects and what doesn't. For optimal results, record yourself regularly under these circumstances and take detailed notes about what you hear. Ideal vehicles for practicing a projecting tone include slow scales and popular Adagio pieces, such as "The Swan," and arrangements for cello of the *Arioso* from Bach's Harpsichord Concerto, BWV 1056, and the *Air* from Orchestral Suite no. 2, BWV 1068, and so on.

CHALLENGE NO. 1A: TONE AND PROJECTION IN THE UPPER REGISTER

How it should sound

Ideally, the tone in the upper register should sound as rich, resonant, and projecting as the tone in any other register on the cello.

What often happens

Some cellists who play with a strong tone in the neck position appear to lose their nerve when playing in the upper register, that is, in thumb position. The pitch veers out of tune, and the tone loses its core. This is because a resonant, projecting tone in the upper register, like a resonant, projecting tone anywhere else on the cello, is a both-handed skill. Some cellists have a hang-up about playing in thumb position: this is probably because the thumb must play on the string alongside the fingers instead of comfortably opposing the fingers around the neck of the cello. This perceived discomfort causes psychological stress. Stress causes homolaterality, and homolaterality causes clumsiness and a poor tone. Faulty intonation often contributes to this poor tone.

Solutions

A contact point that is close to the bridge is even more important in the upper register than in the lower registers, because the higher the pitch, the shorter the string (fig. 4.1). It's important not to get so wrapped up in the intricacies of the left hand that the Tone Triangle is forgotten. It's also vital to pull the bow relatively slowly and to bow relatively close to the frog whenever possible. The goal of a resonant tone should be the starting point for all thumb position work.

Many insecurities about thumb position stem from the inefficient movement of the left arm (and these are only compounded by weak bowing). A number of simple solutions can help.

Curve the left knuckles: Just as flattening the second and third knuckles in the right hand makes for an inefficient bow hold (à la Madame Suggia), flattening out the base knuckles of the left hand restricts the hand's motion and sabotages intonation and fluency in moving between notes. Curved knuckles are flexible; flattened knuckles are stiff. Practice the basic fundamentals of thumb position by curling the left hand into a loose fist, with the relaxed thumb extended alongside the hand. Place the thumb on the A and D harmonics and play these notes with the bow, still keeping the left-hand fingers curled up. Now unfurl the fingers, keeping the base knuckles curved, and play a one-octave D major scale, feeling that the weight of the arm is being channeled through your fingers into the string, giving them the balance, poise, and flexibility they need to move from note to note with vibrato. Always keep your thumb close to your hand, rather than letting it lag behind as you shift up and down; this will help keep your base knuckles curved and improve your ability to move from note to note.

Use autosuggestion: Tell yourself that the efficiency of your Tone Triangle bowing is compelling your left-hand fingers' fluency and accuracy. Also feel that the precision of your left hand influences the projection of your bowing.

Transition smoothly between neck and thumb positions: Much of the common fear of thumb position results from difficulty transitioning there from the neck position. It sometimes helps to remember, as obvious as this sounds, that the string is just a straight line. Your job is to use the most economical arm movements possible to transition between different parts of this straight line with your fingers. Therefore, have your left arm on the same "plane" as you travel from neck position to thumb position and back.

1. Make your left hand into a loose fist with the thumb extended alongside the hand, and using your knuckles, drum up and down the strings of the cello from the nut to the end of the fingerboard and back. Notice how little variation in arm height is truly necessary to make the transition between neck and thumb positions. Economy of the movement is the key to an easy shifting trajectory.
2. Practice the opening of Boccherini's Cello Sonata in A Major, G. 4, as an exercise in this kind of transition (fig. 4.2). Keep your left arm on the same "plane" throughout, that is, support it with enough elevation that you don't have to raise it to get up into the higher position at measure 2. Support and reinforce your left hand's work using the Tone Triangle.

Molto legato, ♩ = 60

vibrate all notes except harmonics

Figure 4.1.   Tone and projection in the upper register

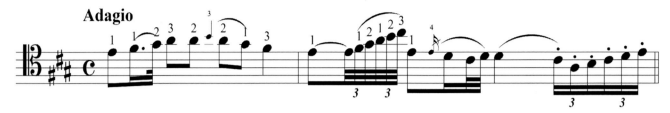

Figure 4.2.   Luigi Boccherini, Cello Sonata in A Major, G. 4, movt. I, mm. 1–2

Coordinate left-hand fluency with string crossings: The following passage from the last movement of Beethoven's Cello Sonata in A Major, op. 69, is difficult for many players because of its speed and the need to cross strings at the same time (fig. 4.3).

It is a good idea to invent exercises to help develop fluency in passages like this.[2] The following exercise takes Beethoven's motive and goes one step further, going up and down the A major scale in modes to work on accuracy and fluency of intonation in combination with seamless string crossing (fig. 4.4). The trick to good string crossing in slurred passages is to prepare the elevation of the right arm for the string crossing well before it actually happens, that is, move the arm to the elevation of the new position in advance of changing string. Practicing the following exercise for even five minutes a day will improve intonation and tone quality in the thumb position. Note that in the Locrian scale, the thumb has to change position in the middle of the scale.

Further suggested studies in the fundamentals of thumb position include A. W. Benoy and L. Sutton's classic book of thumb position études,[3] or for younger players, Rick Mooney's books on the subject.[4] It may also be instructive to invent your own thumb position exercises by taking a book of beginners' pieces and transposing them up an octave into the thumb position.

CHALLENGE NO. 2: CONSISTENCY OF SOUND PRODUCTION IN PHRASING

How it should sound

All movements in cello playing should be in the service of the desired expression, not of the player's convenience. Therefore, under optimal conditions, the player's deep self-listening and thoughtful adjustment of movements mean that the tone of the instrument is the conduit for sensitive music-making. The cellist should be able to "sing" long, undisrupted lines.

What often happens

A surprisingly common error, even in quite advanced playing, is a tone that starts inarticulately, "blossoms" into a louder dynamic, then dies away towards the end. If it were notated, it might look like depicted in figure 4.5. Many musicians call this kind of tone a "banana tone" because of its uneven, curving shape. It isn't exclusively a right-hand problem, because when it happens, the cellist's left hand usually delays vibrato until well after the beginning of the note too. The vibrato then peters out before the end of the note as the cellist prepares for the next note. The bow hand neglects to give a clear "front" to the note, but it attempts to compensate for it by making a crescendo into the middle of the note and then lets the sound die away before the end of the note. The effect is at best irritating, at worst, seasick.

Single notes that swell like this are occasionally acceptable as a special effect when the composer has explicitly notated one. The rest of the time, however, the banana tone is a lazy habit that distracts the listener and detracts from the integrity of the composer's score.

Thoughtless, repetitive banana tones don't work as part of musical expression because the articulation at the beginning of a note—including the left hand's articulation of vibrato—is cardinal to its quality and shape. The attack introduces energy to an instrument, and after this attack, the instrument resonates and the tone takes a pattern of overtone frequencies. An experiment by the electroacoustic composer Pierre Schaeffer (1910–1995),

Figure 4.3.   Ludwig van Beethoven, Cello Sonata in A Major, op. 69, movt. III, mm. 157–58

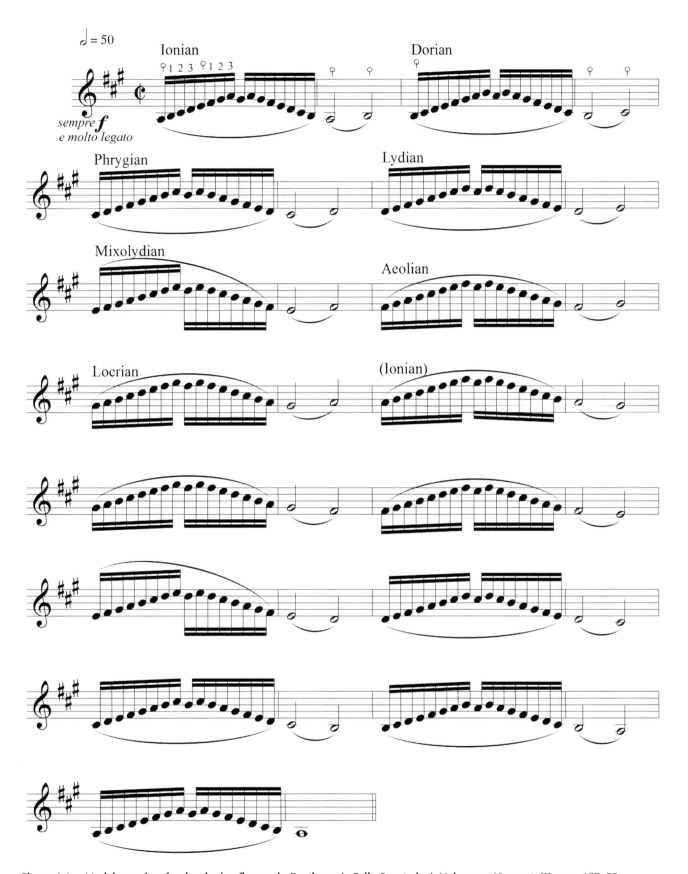

Figure 4.4. Modal exercises for developing fluency in Beethoven's Cello Sonata in A Major, op. 69, movt. III, mm. 157–58

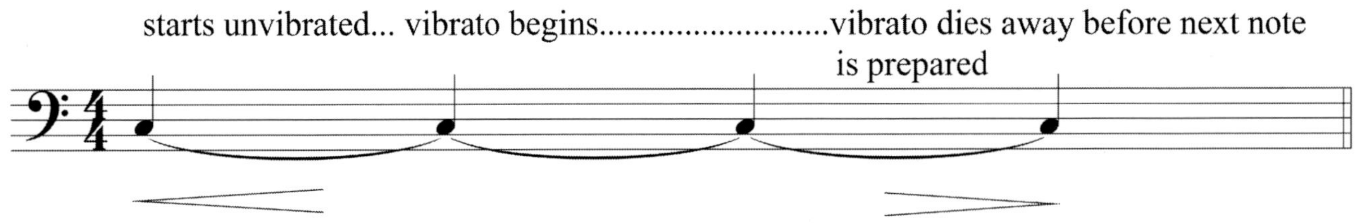

starts unvibrated... vibrato begins..........................vibrato dies away before next note
is prepared

Figure 4.5. Banana tones

in which he took recordings of notes on several instruments and edited out their initial attacks, demonstrates powerfully why attacks are so important. Without the attacks, Schaeffer observed, it was actually difficult to identify the instrument being played.[5] This is just one of the reasons clear articulation is so important.

When this is missing, there will be an impression of dragging, even when the player isn't actually slowing down. In ensembles, players who don't articulate effectively sound as if they're behind, whether they're counting assiduously and watching the conductor or not. This is very common in amateur orchestras and choirs, where players or singers are nervous about being out of tune, and they want to "test" the note before committing to it with vibrato and greater volume. One of the main differences between amateur and professional players—besides obvious factors, such as tone and intonation—is that good professionals don't drag. They commit to notes immediately for the integrity of the ensemble.

Solutions

As always, we can diagnose and solve problems from our starting point of listening to how we sound. It can be a chastening experience to listen closely to your own playing, but daily self-recording and meticulously analyzing what you hear are the first steps in eradicating banana tones. Simply noticing you are doing it is a big step. No one ever set out to make a banana tone—it's simply a careless habit.

Consider the physical means to an end

1. Articulate the beginning of notes by setting yourself up in the strong part of the bow. The lower half of your bow has much more articulatory power than the middle or upper half, and it should thus be the default setting for starting notes. Many cellists never really play at the frog, and it can be a revelation to make this an intentional habit.
2. Articulation and sustaining by both hands are the two best tools for eliminating the banana tone. Movements of the arms should be initiated centrally, through the collarbones and the back. Avoid skimming the bow over the surface of the string by using the Tone Triangle of heavy arm weight, slow bow speed, and a contact point relatively near the bridge.
3. Feel that your strong, evenly pulled bowstroke is *causing* your left arm to vibrate continuously and expressively from the beginning to the end of each note. Feel that your continuous, singing vibrato is *causing* your right arm to bow strongly and evenly all the way through each stroke.
4. Practice the walking fingers exercise (fig. 4.6). As you change finger, direct your arm's weight into the fleshy pad of the "new" finger as you release the old one, while maintaining a continuous vibrato with your arm. Changing note in the middle of the slurs will help you notice if you are habitually stopping vibrato at the beginnings and endings of notes in a manner that coincides with inconsistently pulled bows (thus creating a banana tone).

Adagio ♩ = 40

Use whole bows and continuous vibrato
sempre molto legato

Figure 4.6. Walking fingers exercise

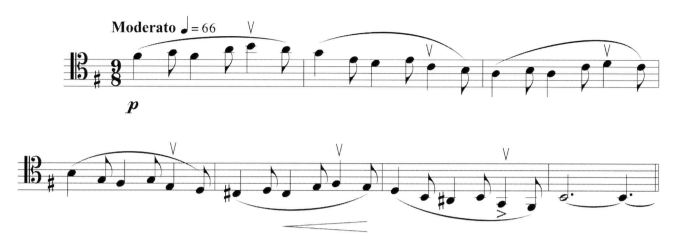

Figure 4.7.   Edward Elgar, Cello Concerto in E Minor, op. 85, movt. I, mm. 15–21

5. Now remove the slurs and notice whether your vibrato is affected. If you catch yourself unthinkingly stopping and starting vibrato when you change pitches, resolve to quit this habit. Start thinking of your arm as the conduit that carries your fingers from note to note rather than thinking of your fingers as independent agents. Your arm will help you move from finger to finger in an arc-like, whole-arm movement as you vibrate. The bow will "activate" your vibrato if its attack is clear and its subsequent movement is sustained by directing the heavy weight of your arm into the string.
6. Invent walking fingers exercises for yourself using different combinations of notes. Incorporate shifts and different kinds of articulations and slurs. Use Louis Feuillard's *Daily Exercises* for ideas.[6]
7. Certain passages in the repertoire may also be used as exercises in walking fingers, such as the main theme of the first movement of the Elgar Cello Concerto (fig. 4.7). Smooth transitions between each note, including consistency of vibrato, are crucial to a singing legato. There must be an intention to create a long, spun-out phrase. The "singingness" of the fingering must em-

power the bowing. Notice that Elgar writes phrasing marks over the top of bowing markings: this implies a long legato line. On the down-bows, the bow speed must be slower and arm weight heavier, whereas on the up-bows, a "light-and-fast" effect will get the bow back to the frog without a surging disruption to the line. Bow changes must be ultra-smooth, using the infinity bows exercise from chapter 2.

Learn from singers

1. When preparing an interpretation, sing through every phrase before you play it to plan the ups and downs of the musical line, the dynamics, and the articulations.
2. When you pick up the cello, cultivate a sense of long lines in your phrasing. Small expressive details are very important, but don't get so lost in them that you lose sight of a phrase's larger structure.
3. Many classic pieces in the cello's repertoire are transcriptions of vocal works. Learn some of them with reference to how the best singers phrase them. One famous example is Fauré's *Après un rêve* (fig. 4.8).

Figure 4.8.   Gabriel Fauré, *Après un rêve* op. 7, no. 1, mm. 1–7, ineffective phrasing

"In a sleep, charmed by your image, I dreamed of happiness, passionate mirage."

Figure 4.9.   Gabriel Fauré, *Après un rêve* op. 7, no. 1, mm. 1–7, vocal original

It's easy to fall into the trap of overusing small crescendi and diminuendi to create micronuances that take away from the expressive sense of a longer line, as in the example below.

We should remember that in Fauré's original, the line also conveys textual meaning (fig. 4.9). Note that the text is mostly sung syllabically, with the notable exception of the long melisma on the second syllable of "mirage." Note also that these seven measures compose one sentence of text. The end of the third measure is not, therefore, the end of the phrase. Now listen to a recording of a great singer, preferably a French one. Notice the contour of the dynamics and phrasing, and where the singer breathes. Try to imitate this kind of phrasing on the cello. It may sound something like figure 4.10.

In other words, there should be a broader sense of cantabile phrasing, in which the first seven measures of the

cello part make up a phrase. The phrase is no longer broken into choppy segments by banana tones. The vibrato is continuous, but continuously varied.

Other vocal works to practice with reference to vocal scores and recordings of singers include transcriptions for cello of Rachmaninoff's *Vocalise* op. 34, no. 14, and Schubert's *Ave Maria* (*Ellens dritter Gesang*, D. 839).

CHALLENGE NO. 3: MOVING FROM NOTE TO NOTE

How it should sound

Ideally, the progression from one note to another should be as clean as possible. A well-planned fingering will help you play a sensitive musical phrase. A well-planned

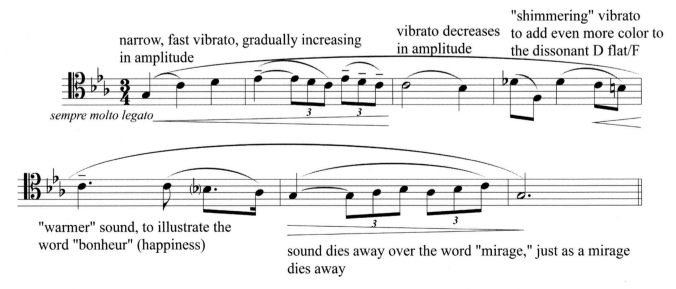

Figure 4.10.   Gabriel Fauré, *Après un rêve* op. 7, no. 1, mm. 1–7, text-inspired phrasing and interpretation

shift will be scarcely perceptible, except on the occasions that an intentionally audible shift contributes to expressiveness in some way.

What often happens

Sometimes a cellist consistently misses shifts, landing on a note out of tune and spoiling the phrase. The cause of the missed shift may be unnecessary tension in the arm at the moment shifting begins, or poor positioning of the arm, or a problem with hearing the goal note "in the mind's ear." Even when a shift is efficiently executed, a poorly planned fingering can result in an inexpressive

audible slide. Sometimes, furthermore, an otherwise attractive phrase is disrupted by a carelessly executed shift.

Solutions

Work on the fundamentals of expressive fingering and expressive shifting every day to improve your efficiency. When planning fingerings and shifts, look for those that will most effectively help your intended expression. Again, it is desirable to imitate singers: when working on an intentionally audible shift, sing the passage several different ways. Choose a speed and style of shift that sounds the most like what a singer would do.

Figure 4.11.   Modern shifts and old-fashioned shifts

Using the infinity symbol shifting motion from the warm-up exercises in chapter 2, practice the following exercises in "modern" and "old-fashioned" audible shifts from first to fourth position (fig. 4.11). (The "old-fashioned" shift was common among cellists of the first generation of recorded musicians, i.e., Casals and his contemporaries.) In "modern" shifts, you shift on the "new" finger (that is, the finger you have decided to play the second note with). In "old-fashioned" shifts, you shift on the "old" finger and put the "new" finger down only at the end of the shift as you land on the second note. In all cases, the shifts should be deliberately audible.

1. Repeat this exercise on all the strings.
2. Tips for efficient fourth-position shifting: support your left arm with elevation—a guiding rule should be to ask yourself whether your arm is elevated enough to transport you easily beyond the neck position. When you are moving to fourth position, use your thumb to guide your hand there by letting it graze the hollow where the back of the cello's neck joins its body. Some inexperienced teachers teach students to find fourth position by slamming the side of the hand into the body of the cello. The problem with this isn't just the unpleasant thumping noise it creates, but that you

can't shift up any farther than fourth position without having to hoist the arm up in an uncomfortable and inefficient manner. This can cause you to miss shifts. To find the right level of elevation for your arm, practice the knuckle-drumming exercise from section 1a of this chapter.

Continuing to use infinity symbol shifting, also practice shifts of an octave using the same kind of fingering pattern (with only "modern" shifts this time) (fig. 4.12).

1. "Feel" your shifts with the bow. Aim for the sensation of "pulling through" the shift with the legato stroke of your bow.
2. As a variation on this exercise, practice the same exercise using two-octave shifts instead of one-octave shifts.

Expression vs. transportation in shifting

There are two types of audible shifts. Under certain conditions, making a shift audible on purpose can contribute to the expression of a phrase, hence "shift of expression." Making an audible slide for no other reason than to get

Figure 4.12. Octave shifts

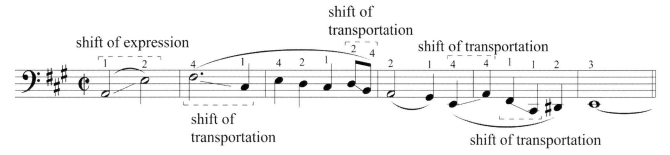

Figure 4.13. Ludwig van Beethoven, Cello Sonata in A Major, op. 69, movt. I, mm. 1–6, shifts of expression vs. shifts of transportation

the hand from one position to another, however, is just a "shift of transportation." Audible shifts are part of the art of expressive interpretation, but we can be smart about where to place them and when to suppress them.

1. In an example from the opening of Beethoven's Cello Sonata in A Major, op. 69, it is traditional (and effective) to get from the first note to the second with a shift of expression, which we may execute in either modern or old-fashioned style, according to taste (fig. 4.13). This reflects the way we might sing this passage. But the fingering shown is planned according to convenience rather than expression, and this forces "shifts of transportation."

2. There are two ways to avoid an unnecessary audible shift. The first is to lighten the weight of the right arm in the string, as briefly and imperceptibly as possible, to disguise the shift. This sometimes works well, but in a passage like this with a lot of shifts, it can problematically disrupt the flow of the legato line. The second way to deemphasize the shifts is to arrange the fingering so that shifts will take place over the smallest possible interval—preferably a half-step. When you can't do this, arrange your fingering and bowing so that you change bow at the same time as you shift, then shift as fast as possible. You can minimize the audibility of your shifts in this Beethoven passage by planning your fingerings and bowings like this (fig. 4.14):

3. Sometimes it's tempting to make an audible shift over a bow change. This is another lazy habit that takes expression away from the line. The opening of "The Swan" is often played with two audible shifts in the very first measure (fig. 4.15). Only one is a shift of expression. To avoid the shift of transportation, you could try half-shifting, half-stretching your hand to get from first finger B to fourth finger E, and also infinitesimally lightening your arm's weight during the bow change to minimize any audible sliding.

4. Too much of a good thing: avoid the temptation to overstate the sentimentality of Romantic salon pieces by injecting too many shifts of expression. In this excerpt from Fauré's *Élégie* op. 24, there are three places one might intentionally add an audible shift to the phrase (fig. 4.16). Choosing one or two might be stylistically appropriate and emotionally affecting, but to use all three would quickly become distracting and even annoying to the audience's ears.

Although it is permissible in highly Romantic music to play more audible shifts than you would in Beethoven's Cello Sonata op. 69, in a passage like this it's best to pick one shift and minimize the others by stretching rather than shifting between the notes, or by lightening the amount of arm weight for the split second in which you shift.

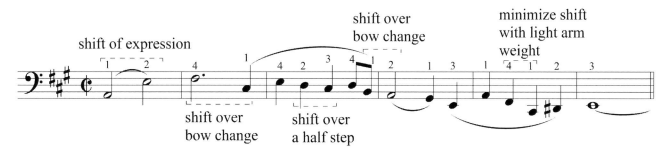

Figure 4.14. Ludwig van Beethoven, Cello Sonata in A Major, op. 69, movt. I, mm. 1–6, how to avoid ineffective audible shifts

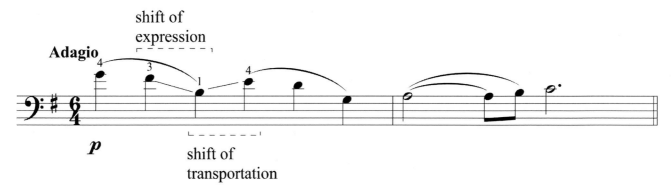

Figure 4.15.   Camille Saint-Saëns, *Carnival of the Animals*, movt. XIII, "The Swan," mm. 1–2

Figure 4.16.   Gabriel Fauré, *Élégie* op. 24, mm. 30–31

SUMMARY OF WHOLE-BODY SOLUTIONS TO THE CHALLENGES OF CELLO PLAYING

• Effectiveness in cello playing relies upon the cultivation of efficient physical habits. Therefore, expressive music-making is dependent on a combination of both-handed physical actions that create pitches, phrases, and colors.

• To create a projecting tone, we must combine the adjustable components of contact point, arm weight, and bow speed. But the Tone Triangle alone will not work without the support of components such as clean intonation and sensitive vibrato.

• The next component in creating effective interpretations is to be able to move from one note to another in a thoughtful and sensitive way. Fingerings and shifts should be planned for maximum effectiveness, not for convenience. The only time a shift should be audible is when it's done on purpose for expressive reasons.

Chapter Five

Habits for Efficient Practice

"How should I practice?" is the most common question students ask their teachers, followed closely by "How much should I practice?" The question should really be "What should I accomplish when I practice?"

So much of the practice done even by quite advanced musicians is inefficient because of a common misconception that practice should be measured by hours rather than by achievements. Furthermore, much of what cellists do in the practice room reinforces mistakes and bad habits, and that doesn't prepare them for performance.

SETTING CLEAR GOALS

The ability to perform successfully should be the overarching goal of efficient practice. Under that arch are various broad subgoals, including:

• Maintaining existing skills.
• Learning new skills to establish neural pathways in our brains that will enable us to improve.[1]
• Unlearning mistakes and inefficient playing methods, and creating new and stronger neural pathways to override them. This is, unsurprisingly, much more difficult than learning a new skill for the first time.[2]
• Learning musical scores, both at and away from the cello.
• Preparing for performance.

The idea of preparing for performance is probably the most neglected part of practice, even though performing in public is often an anxiety-inducing activity. For some performers, the symptoms of stage fright can be quite incapacitating. And yet, many cellists continue to invest all their inspirations in one dream performance, merely hoping that it will go well rather than making performing part of every practice day. It's too late to start worrying about how you'll deal with nerves when you're sitting in the greenroom, about to walk out on stage.

It therefore makes sense always to practice as if you were performing for others. Anything less—fooling about with a weak sound, tolerating errors and poor intonation, repeatedly running whole pieces without fixing troublesome sections, learning new pieces mechanistically—is a lazy habit and a waste of time. Instead, you should pretend you're in front of an audience from the first second of your practice.[3]

The ideal practice day probably doesn't exist, since there are never perfect conditions, enough time, or enough energy. It's still possible to accomplish a lot in even short sessions, however. In general, efficient practice should include at least some of the following categories:

1. Cross-Lateral Exercises
2. Fundamentals
3. Score Study and Analysis
4. Listening and Modeling
5. Score Preparation at the Cello
6. Mindful Repetition
7. Memorization
8. Self-Recording and Evaluation
9. Performing Every Day

Habit No. 1 has already been covered in chapter 2. Remember that cross-lateral, infinity, and tapping exercises are useful at any time of the day, even away from the cello and the practice room, to improve concentration and energy.

HABIT NO. 2: FUNDAMENTALS

In many ways, Habit No. 2 is an extension of Habit No. 1. The practice of fundamentals—the basic elements of our art—starts with the exercises in cross-laterality, long tones, breathing, and shifting (from chapter 2). It also includes exercises in bowstrokes and fingering patterns, such as those in Louis Feuillard's *Daily Exercises*. Practiced mindfully, a Feuillard exercise or two each day can be a refresher course in efficient movement. After working on these basics, a daily fundamentals workload should include major and minor scales in various bowings, arpeggios in various bowings and inversions, scales in thirds, sixths, and octaves, focusing on the principles of effective tone production, harmonic intonation, vibrato, and other considerations from earlier chapters of this book.

Other scales, arpeggios, and double-stops

Scales practice shouldn't be restricted to the diatonic ones, however. Now that the early works of Stravinsky and Bartók, Kodály's Sonata for Solo Cello op. 8, Debussy's String Quartet in G Minor, op. 10, and Cello Sonata in D Minor, and Ravel's String Quartet in F Major are a century old or more, it seems strange that nondiatonic scales aren't part of the standard cello scales repertoire. See the appendix for suggested fingerings for pentatonic, hexatonic, and octatonic scales, and arpeggios in augmented triads and various seventh chords.[4] It also makes sense to practice double-stops in perfect fourths and perfect fifths, since these are found relatively often in repertoire and are typically difficult to play in tune.

Études

In addition to practicing scales daily, cellists should keep difficult études in their regular repertoire. David Popper's *High School of Cello Playing* op. 73—reputedly the inspiration for some of the pyrotechnics in Prokofiev's Symphony-Concerto op. 125—and Alfredo Piatti's *12 Caprices* op. 25 are compositionally interesting and satisfying to play. Between them, they cover virtually all the techniques cellists need to master the canonic repertoire of the eighteenth and nineteenth centuries.

Long warm-ups: essential or overrated?

The practice of fundamentals is so essential to artistry that if you find yourself with only twenty minutes of practice time for the entire day, you should work on them, not on repertoire. Fundamentals are the foundations of musicianship and expressiveness in performance. It's important to note, though, that fundamentals shouldn't take a long time at the beginning of your practice day. Too many hardworking cellists waste their time, energy, and concentration on extended fundamentals sessions—sometimes using as much as the first two hours of the day's practice time—that don't necessarily help their performance and can tire them out before they've

had a chance to work on learning and polishing scores. A recent scientific study concluded that large amounts of stretching warm-ups don't improve the performance of athletes, but they may even be counterproductive.[5] It stands to reason that there may be parallels for musicians, and that excessive fundamentals workouts prior to a performance may not be effective. Try playing only a short fundamentals warm-up as your first practice of the day—fifteen minutes of long tones with vibrato, or some slow scales—and interspersing the rest of your practice day with short bursts of double-stops, études, shifting exercises, and so on.

Cleaning your hands

In many ways, it can actually be more efficient to practice the bulk of your fundamentals at the *end* of your practice day, for example, after a long orchestra rehearsal, where efficiency of movement and resonance of tone might not have been top priorities. One of my teachers used to describe this practice as "cleaning your hands." An evening session on fundamentals can be like a reset button for your technique, away from the multitasking and distractions of the life of a professional. It takes discipline to sit down with the cello when you are tired and your concentration is weakened, but if you make this a habit, you can find yourself looking forward to it as an almost meditative practice.

Concert-hall tone

Of course, fundamentals practice is only useful if it's approached with the same energy and commitment that you'd bring to performing repertoire. Aim at all times to use the same projecting, resonant sound that you would need in a large concert hall. It can be difficult to anticipate how to do this if you don't often have the chance to practice in such a venue, because producing a resonant tone in the acoustics of a practice room is much easier. Because of this, you should seek out large practice spaces whenever possible. Churches, for example, may permit musicians to practice in their premises in exchange for performing at religious services. If you can't access a large practice space, be aware of the difference in acoustics between a small room and a large hall, and use the parameters of the Tone Triangle to produce concert-hall tone. Even if this sounds slightly harsh under your ear, remember that the core of a resonant tone will project, but much of the harshness will not.

It is a mistake to play any exercise in fundamentals mechanically, as if it were not related to music. Although fundamentals are essential for maintaining efficient playing skills, I make no distinction between fundamentals and repertoire when it comes to practicing emotional expression. Both are an opportunity to work on cross-laterality and breathing to produce the most resonant possible tone and a logical trajectory from note to note through efficient fingering and shifting. These, after all, are the basic materials of our ability to move the hearts of our audiences.

HABIT NO. 3: SCORE STUDY AND ANALYSIS

Studying a score is a way to grasp the big picture of a composition—that is, the large-scale forms and structures—of what you're trying to accomplish in performance. Big-picture learning has been shown to help medical students prepare for exams.[6] Just as a doctor has to memorize and juggle many facts as part of a broader purpose of diagnosing and treating illness, a cellist must know exactly what is happening thematically, harmonically, and structurally, and how the other parts fit in with the cello part, when the composition is for more than one player.

An overview of an entire work in its full-score form is vital to learning a new piece. Too many advanced cellists start to learn a new piece at the cello with only the cello part in front of them, without even consulting the full score, and this is an inefficient way to learn.

Why study the score without a recording?

In his "Advice for Young Musicians," an article that is as relevant today as it was in 1850, Robert Schumann counsels, "You must get to a point where you can understand the music from the page."[7] We can see a fictionalized example of this heightened level of musicianship in the film *Amadeus*, where the jealous composer Antonio Salieri leafs through a stack of Mozart's manuscripts, "hearing" snippets of concerti, symphonies, sonatas, and operas. I recommend getting into the habit of studying the score first without the aid of a recording as an exercise in ear training of the highest level.

Now that so much music is freely available online, many cellists' libraries consist largely of printouts on flimsy photocopy paper. These are undeniably convenient, but most free downloads are old-fashioned, heavily edited versions of compositions. It's better to invest in modern scholarly performers' editions, such as those by G. Henle and Bärenreiter, because they reproduce composers' notes and markings more reliably. At an advanced level, moreover, it's better to decide on one's own bowings, fingerings, and expressive markings than to accept those of an editor. Certainly, the best scores are not cheap, but the quality of the scholarship—not to mention the paper—means they will last a lifetime.

Motives and harmony

Once you have learned the broader structural plan of the movements of a composition, it's time to identify thematic and motivic materials and their harmonic transitions and transformations over the course of a movement. This will help with memorization later in the learning process. It's also essential to learn the other players' parts just as thoroughly as you learn the cello part. This helps create a dialogue of equals and a convincing group sound.

The practice of score study can be done with nothing more than a score and a pencil, though it may be useful to have a book on music analysis, such as William Caplin's *Classical Form*,[8] at the ready. (If the musical language of the composition is postdiatonic, it may be preferable to use a text such as Joseph N. Straus's *Introduction to Post-Tonal Theory*.[9])

The first step should be to make a formal, thematic, and harmonic analysis of each movement. If the movement is in sonata-allegro form, for example, write in where the exposition, development, and recapitulation occur, and also smaller subsections, such as introductions, transitions, and codas. Identify and label the thematic and motivic materials. Analyze the structure of the phrases: What is the harmonic structure? Where are the cadences? What keys do the themes go through in the different sections of the music? Where are the high and low points of phrases? Where is the culminating high point of the movement? What are the composer's dynamic and articulation markings, and how do they contribute to the drama of the movement? Internalize and memorize the harmonic and structural plans of a movement, because this will help you memorize the smaller-scale details later.

A brief formal, thematic, and harmonic analysis of *Bourrée II* from J. S. Bach, Cello Suite no. 4 in E-flat Major, BWV 1010. This movement is in a rounded binary (or simple ternary) form, with two clear contrasting sections. There is no true modulation, though Bach briefly tonicizes ii and V in the B section (fig. 5.1).

At first glance, the movement appears to be monothematic, since the melodic contour of the A section theme is very similar to that of the B section theme. But if we separate the two voices of the counterpoint, we see that whereas the contour of the bassline is in largely ascending motion in the A sections, it descends in the B section. This is where we can get some of our sense of thematic contrast in an interpretation (fig. 5.2).

Figure 5.1. Johann Sebastian Bach, Cello Suite no. 4 in E-flat Major, BWV 1010, Bourrée II, formal and chordal analysis

Figure 5.2. Johann Sebastian Bach, Cello Suite no. 4 in E-flat Major, BWV 1010, Bourrée II, thematic analysis

Sing and plan

The next step in the score study process is to sing the cello part, and the other parts if the work is for more than one player. Don't be discouraged if you aren't a good singer: it doesn't matter if you have a weak vocal tone or a limited range, though you should aim for perfect rhythmic accuracy. Taking the composer's metronome markings, sing and conduct to the beat of a metronome so that the goal tempo is always in your mind. From the earliest stages of score-learning, sing with as much expression as possible, planning the high and low points of the phrases and scrupulously observing the composer's dynamic and articulation markings. Away from the restrictions of the cello and your technique, you can plan an expressive ideal.

Breathing and the natural ebbs and flows of the human voice should be the models for phrasing on the cello. Notice the consonants and vowels that you instinctively use for articulations, and remember them when it comes to deciding on bowstrokes and articulations later. For example, percussive consonants such as "ta-ka-ta-ka-ta-ka" for a marcato passage, "id-ill-id-ill-id-ill" for a détaché run, or a melismatic "ah" for a long legato phrase convey nuances that will affect your choice of bowings, bowstrokes, and fingerings.

If you have studied moveable-*do* solfège, it is a good idea also to use it for singing through repertoire, because it will help you integrate theoretical concepts such as intervals and harmony with your interpretation.

Don't just sing the cello part, however. Sing all the other parts until you know them as well as you know your own, and make study of the full score part of a daily routine, even when you know the piece very well, to check that you're observing all the composer's directions for articulations, dynamics, and so on. This will become as important in practice as it is in rehearsal.

HABIT NO. 4: LISTENING AND MODELING

Recordings as teachers

Listening to recordings is an invaluable exercise in sound modeling. Just as surgeons in a teaching hospital observe other surgeons performing difficult procedures so that they can learn new techniques, cellists should listen to the great cellists—and chamber ensembles and orchestras—for ideas and inspiration. Imagine that the great musicians of the past and present are your teachers, and learn as much as possible from their models of sound and phrasing.

Even if you aren't privileged to play on a first-class instrument like the ones most of the top players use, you can still aim to produce their heightened levels of energy and projection. If you listen closely enough, you can get to the point of being able to tell which fingerings and bowings the cellist is using, even when there is no video.

When preparing an interpretation, it's useful to listen to as many recordings of the piece as possible. One main reason is to compare the interpretations and mine them for ideas—imitation is, after all, the sincerest form of flattery. Observe the methods the artist uses for tone color, use of vibrato, high and low points of phrases, achieving contrast and surprise, and so on.

Performance histories

Another reason for comparative listening is to understand the evolution of cello playing since the earliest days of recording and the need for sensitivity to period performance. One benefit of daily deep listening is, of course, the chance to hear the artistry of cellists at the top of their profession, but it can also help with the study of historically informed performance practice. In many cases, composers living within the age of recording technology made recordings of their own compositions. Not many of them were cellists themselves—some were pianists and conductors who accompanied the cellists of their time—and they presumably endorsed those cellists' interpretations. These recordings can be primary documents in building a stylistically conscientious interpretation.[10] Consider, for example, Beatrice Harrison's recording of Edward Elgar's Cello Concerto op. 85, with Elgar himself conducting,[11] or Zara Nelsova's recording of Ernest Bloch's "Prayer" from *Jewish Life* with the composer at the piano.[12]

Aside from offering us the chance to hear composers performing their own works, historic recordings also let us hear how fashions in cello performance have changed, so that we may contemplate their evolution. Nowhere is this more evident than in Bach performance, one of the most contentious fields of interpretation. If we compare three recordings of the Sarabande from Bach's Cello Suite no. 6 in D Major, BWV 1012, those of Anner Bylsma (1993),[13] Pierre Fournier (ca. 1961–63),[14] and Julius Klengel (1927),[15] we can hear exemplars from three completely different schools, and eras, of cello playing.

Bylsma, a leading proponent of the modern, historically informed performance practice movement, is using a five-string violoncello piccolo from around the turn of the eighteenth century and a modern replica of a Baroque bow (fig. 5.3). Having five strings—C, G, D, A, E—permits him to play all the notes of the chords in measures 2, 5, and 6, a feat that is normally not possible on the modern four-string cello. His strings, which are made of gut, are tuned to A = 415, and this creates a much more

Figure 5.3.   Johann Sebastian Bach, Cello Suite no. 6 in D Major, BWV 1012, Sarabande, mm. 1–8, Anner Bylsma's interpretation

open, less bright resonance than a modern four-string cello with steel strings can produce. In his interpretation, all the three-, four-, and five-note chords are broken slowly in an arpeggiated manner, as are one or two of the double-stops. Bylsma often releases his bow after the initial articulation of a note, causing a slight diminuendo.

Going back thirty years to the Pierre Fournier recording, we may reasonably assume Fournier was not trying to recreate the performance practices of Bach's time (fig. 5.4). His playing here typifies the heroic, sostenuto tone, wide vibrato, and assertive articulations of many virtuosi of the middle of the twentieth century. He breaks the chords quickly in a "two plus two" manner, and in the ones in measures 2 and 6, which don't fall within the human handspan on the modern four-string cello, he plays two double-stops separated by a very quick shift, allowing him to play all the notes. His tempo is slow, without much rubato.

Neither Bylsma's nor Fournier's performances of Bach sound alien to modern ears today, though some might find Fournier's mid-century romantic intensity dated. But what happens if we go back another thirty years to Klengel's recording of the Sarabande, which appears here in his own arrangement for cello and piano (fig. 5.5)? Disregarding for now that the nineteenth-century practice of creating piano accompaniments for Bach's solo works is unfashionable or even derided today, the most striking thing about Klengel's interpretation is his practice of sliding markedly and deliberately from note to note. Admittedly, Klengel was sixty-eight years old when he made this recording, and his glissandi were more typical of an older generation of cellists, but we can tell from other digitally remastered historical performances that this had once been a widespread practice.

Whose playing comes closest to Bach's intentions? Is it Bylsma, the modern scholar-performer, with his supe-

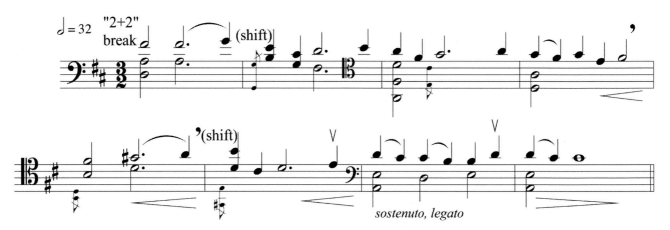

Figure 5.4.   Johann Sebastian Bach, Cello Suite no. 6 in D Major, BWV 1012, Sarabande, mm. 1–8, Pierre Fournier's interpretation

Figure 5.5. Johann Sebastian Bach, Cello Suite no. 6 in D Major, BWV 1012, Sarabande, mm. 1–8, Julius Klengel's interpretation

rior knowledge of Baroque manuscript sources and playing techniques? Is it Fournier, whose direct emotional approach virtually jumps out at us from the stereo speakers? Or is it Klengel, a lifelong resident of Bach's adopted city of Leipzig—and one of the last exponents of a much older tradition of German cello playing, before politics, war, mass murder, and emigration fragmented the previously unbroken lineage of European musical inheritance? The answer is that there can be no answer.

The open-minded comparison of printed scores with recorded interpretations is a vast topic, and one that can raise more questions than answers. Since technology has now advanced to the point that a vast number of recordings are instantly available, it is easier than ever to form an overview of the history of cello repertoire interpretation. Listen to everything available, engage in lively debates with colleagues, be receptive to all influences, and enjoy the ever-changing process of shaping an interpretation.

HABIT NO. 5: SCORE PREPARATION AT THE CELLO

Once you have studied a score and any available recordings thoroughly, it's time to sight-read at the cello. This isn't sight-reading in the sense of never having seen the music before, obviously. Instead, you'll be coming to the music with your goals for effective phrasing already planned out from your previous singing sessions. This way, you can experiment with the fingerings, bowings, articulations, dynamics, tone colors, shifts, and so on that best serve your interpretative aspirations.

Play as you sang

Once you have planned your phrases and nuances with singing, play the material on the cello, trying to imitate the expression you used when you sang. Following the suggestions in chapter 4, plan fingerings that avoid unnecessary audible shifts and a bow distribution that allows you to stress the important beats of the measure and not the weak beats. It's inefficient to do this the other way around, that is, to plan your phrasing around convenient fingerings, bowings, or shifts. Some cellists approach pieces by learning the notes so they can "just play" them, regardless of whether their chosen fingerings, bowings, and so on really express the phrase well. To practice this kind of inefficient, thoughtless note-crunching is to accept physical or psychological blocks to improvement. Why waste time teaching yourself bad habits that you will have to undo later in order to improve your performance? Instead, always make expressiveness the starting point and faithfulness to the score a main goal. This is why singing before playing is so important.

Making chamber music by yourself

When you are preparing a composition for more than one player, go back to singing through all of the parts in the score. One challenging but useful practice tip for ensemble music is to play a few measures of the cello part while singing another part. Singing and playing simultaneously has its challenges, but with perseverance it can greatly enrich the experience of learning repertoire.

Slow practice isn't everything

It's almost inevitable that in the early stages of score preparation, you won't be able to play a piece up to tempo. When this happens, try to commit as much as possible to your planned phrasing and articulation, even under tempo. Slow practice has its place, naturally: it helps with learning notes, analyzing movement, and releasing tension,[16] but it's not always productive to think of it as a cure-all, or that you'll be able to play a piece accurately up to tempo just because you can play it slowly. Work towards your goal tempo as soon as possible, because the type of bowstrokes and finger actions you'll use at a fast tempo will be very different from those you were using in the slow tempo.

As you do this, the metronome has the potential to be your best friend. And yet, how many of us are misusing it? The common practice of pushing the tempo up notch by notch until the goal tempo is reached is, in fact, a very good way of training yourself always to be slightly too slow and behind the beat. This is particularly problematic on the cello, because our strings are thicker than those of the violin and viola, and they have a slower response time. A smarter way of using the metronome is to vary the tempo back and forth.

Two steps forward, one step back

If you need to play a difficult passage at 100 beats per minute but can only play it at 80, try setting the metronome to 75. Play several repetitions of the passage, or a small section of it, as accurately and expressively as possible, pinpointing and fixing any mistakes along the way. Then, set the metronome to 85 and repeat the passage. It may be a bit of a scramble at first, so practice it until it becomes slightly easier. Now put the metronome back to 80, and feel how much easier it is to play at that tempo. Congratulate yourself—you just taught yourself to play faster!

Next, set the metronome to 90, then back to 85, then forward to 95, back to 90, and so on, until you can play the passage at 105. If you can play this passage accurately at a *faster* tempo than your goal, you'll know you've mastered it.

By the same token, you can also master extremely slow tempi by practicing with a slower metronome marking than you need. In a piece such as the "Louange à l'éternité de Jésus" from Olivier Messiaen's *Quatuor pour la fin du temps*, where the composer's metronome marking is 44 to the sixteenth note, practicing with the metronome at 40 will lessen the difficulty of sustaining the line at 44.

HABIT NO. 6: MINDFUL REPETITION

The concept of learning by repetition goes in and out of fashion in music pedagogy. Its critics claim that it creates human robots who obsessively learn pieces of information without truly understanding their meaning. But learning by repetition is only mindless if it's done badly. For example, if you decide to repeat a difficult section one hundred times in the hopes of fixing it, you are merely teaching yourself to play it incorrectly at least ninety-nine times, by which time the bad habit will be permanent. But if you make sure you only ever practice repetitions of *correct* skills, repetition becomes one of the most important tools for self-teaching.

Shinichi Suzuki, the great violin pedagogue, compared learning music to learning to talk.[17] He observed that all small children make mistakes and mispronunciations in their speech, but through persistence, many repetitions, and loving correction from adults, they learn to speak coherently. It's the same with learning skills on the cello. Don't be ashamed of sounding bad on the first few attempts, because everyone sounds bad when they first try to do something. The important issue is to analyze as closely as possible what is going wrong and then find creative, effective ways to correct it.

Choose a goal

You must first have a well-defined idea of what you're trying to self-teach. Common practice-room goals include building speed, performing difficult sections of music accurately and reliably, and polishing intonation. A sound model, such as an audio or video recording of a great cellist, helps to create ambitious goals. Approach these goals with the performance-level energy and commitment of one of the great cellists, no matter how clumsy your execution is at the beginning.

Identify the problem, test out solutions

The next step is to isolate the problem passage—a phrase containing a big shift, for example—and pinpoint the exact moment at which your physical movements start to sabotage the success of the shift. (Using a large mirror may help identify this, as may a homemade video recording.) Next, experiment with possible solutions—a more streamlined movement of the left arm, a conscious relaxation of the arm's muscles before attempting the shift, a more confident bowstroke to support and reinforce the left arm's movement, a more natural spacing of the left hand's fingers during the shift, and so on. It may take many experiments to find one that works.

Replicate your success

Now for the hard part: trying to replicate what went right, both the result and the process that got you there. Many cellists unwittingly train themselves to miss problematic sections when they practice them incorrectly, over and over, in the hopes that one of these times, they'll improve. In reality, the only thing that will improve a trouble spot is isolating exactly what went wrong, solving the problem, knowing how you solved it, and repeating it the successful way. Anything else is merely ingraining an inefficient habit. One method for creating a pattern of success is to compose your own études; this will be addressed in a later chapter.

Variation

The principles of alternation and variation are very important to productivity. A danger of repetitive practice is that it can become boring, slow-paced, and unproductive. Keep practice sessions fast-paced and varied by mostly working on short sections for short amounts of time, then switching back and forth between other sections. Research by the clarinetist and music psychologist Christine Carter has demonstrated that musicians retain learned concepts far better when they use a randomized practice schedule than when they practice concepts in consecutive "blocks" of time.[18]

Running pieces repeatedly is inefficient

This is also why repeatedly running long sections, or entire pieces, is not an efficient use of repetition. The occasional full run-through can help you understand how to pace the dramatic ups and downs of the large-scale formal plan, and to isolate trouble spots, but on the whole, running pieces uses a lot of time for not much effect. It's also an excellent way to ingrain mistakes, poor intonation, and other careless habits. Some nervous players are tempted to run their concert programs four or five times a day in the days or weeks leading up to an important concert to build stamina, but this is really not necessary. When you are performing for others, adrenaline gives you all the stamina you need.

HABIT NO. 7: MEMORIZATION

Unlike brass, woodwind, and percussion players, string players are expected to perform concertos and most unaccompanied pieces from memory, unless the composition has extremely complicated post-tonal language. Memorization is one of those aspects of performance that are easy for some but utterly terrifying for others. In spite of this, many teachers and students treat memorization as a haphazard process that you're either naturally good at or you're not.

And yet, memorization is normal for the human brain. Everyone memorizes vast amounts of information without even thinking about it, and the conscious practice of memorization can develop our ability even further.

There are two broad types of memorization practice: deliberate and nondeliberate. The nondeliberate kind is what you pick up automatically and inadvertently while working on something else; it's when you walk out of the practice room humming the catchy melody you were just practicing without necessarily intending to memorize it. It includes the muscle memory you build by learning what a passage "feels like." Muscle memory is useful in the memorization process, but it should not be the only method you use because it isn't completely reliable. Many cellists make the embarrassing mistake, when they reach the recapitulation of a piece in sonata-allegro form, of taking an unthinking wrong turn by playing the second theme in its original key from the exposition. Their muscle memory reminds them what playing a certain theme feels like, but under stress they can only play the theme by feel in one key. This can fluster even the calmest of performers and result in stopping mid-performance.

Theoretical/analytical memorization

Deliberate memorization is a feature of repetitive learning. It starts at a big-picture level with score study. A far-off goal of the first penciled annotations in a full score—"Second theme, recapitulated in the home key," "Transition, modulates to the dominant"—is to internalize the formal and key structures of a movement to the extent that you know where you are in the score at all times. It doesn't matter if you don't have a photographic memory that allows you to visualize what the pages of the score look like. It's far more important to have an analytical awareness of what is going on in the music at all times.

Once you've sorted out the thematic, harmonic, and structural components of a movement according to the logic of music theory and analysis, it's time to start memorizing short sections and then start putting them together. Analyze the phrase structures of the thematic material. For music of the Classical era (it can also apply to some compositions from earlier and later eras in music history), William Caplin offers the useful distinction between two main types of phrase: the sentence and the period. In a sentence, a basic idea is followed by a contrasting idea at the start of the phrase, develops through a continuation section, and ends with a cadence. The period, by contrast, has antecedent–consequent structure.[19] When you understand these components of a phrase, it's easier to memorize the ups and downs of the line, the rhythms, and the implied harmonies.

In this example of a sentence from Beethoven's Cello Sonata in G Minor, op. 5, no. 2, the first two measures establish the "germ" of an idea (fig. 5.6). The second two measures repeat the idea, but on higher pitches—for greater emphasis or greater harmonic tension?—and the

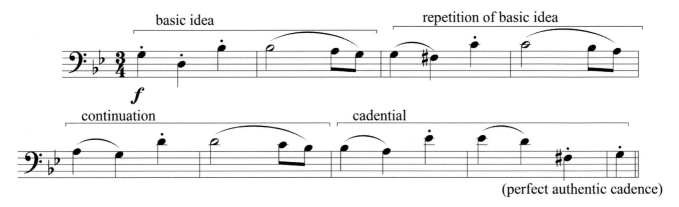

Figure 5.6. Ludwig van Beethoven, Cello Sonata in G Minor, op. 5, no. 2, movt. I, mm. 69–78, sentence structure

third iteration carries it somewhere further, towards a cadence, and later a transition.

The three-part structure of so many musical phrases is no accident, since many composers had a superstitious interest in the number three. Threes are everywhere in European literature, folklore, and music: the Masonic numerical symbolism in Mozart's works; the golden, silver, and lead caskets in Shakespeare's *The Merchant of Venice*; not to mention the multitude of fairy tales where the hero's journey takes him on a road that forks three ways. The first way, being too easy, is an obvious trap; the second is a less obvious trap; and the third way, which initially seems unlikely, leads the hero out of a dark forest, through a maze, or through a hedge of thorns to the castle and the princess. This kind of narrative imagery can not only help with the memorization of a sentence, but it can also work towards an imaginative interpretation.

Period structure is usually more symmetrical than sentence structure, and this can have some bearing on how we interpret and memorize it. In this example of period structure from the second theme in the first movement of Rachmaninoff's Cello Sonata, the sense of bittersweet conflict comes from the surprise syncopated D in the consequent, which disrupts the symmetry (fig. 5.7). Other features to analyze and internalize include the mixed mode of the basic idea: the key is D major, but B-flat—the flatted sixth degree, otherwise known as *le* in moveable-*do* solfège, and borrowed from the minor mode—adds pathos to the melody and harmony. The contrasting idea, presented in ascending motion in the antecedent, descends toward a perfect cadence in the consequent. The rising-falling shape of the structured melodic movement is the basic outline for memorization; the smaller details of modes and rhythms are added as nuances of interpretative emotion.

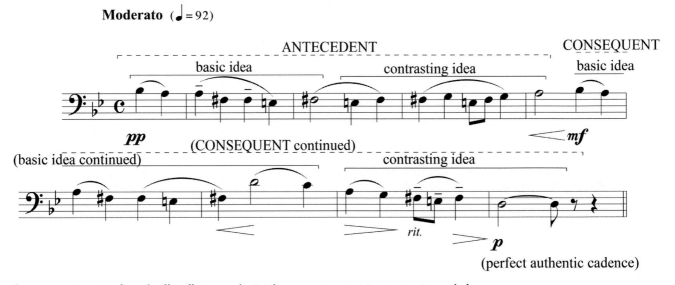

Figure 5.7. Serge Rachmaninoff, Cello Sonata in G Minor, op. 19, movt. I, mm. 61–69, period structure

When you first form an interpretation of phrases like the sentence and period above, begin, as always, with singing. Conduct yourself—would you take the Rachmaninoff example in four, or perhaps in a broad two?—and chant the rhythms, using a neutral syllable like "tah" to feel the swing of a melody. Now add pitches, using moveable-*do* solfège if you know it, to internalize the intervallic and chordal relations. Sing the phrase again, using the invented syllables of your choice—the Beethoven example might call for percussive consonants, such as Ts and Ds, whereas the more legato Rachmaninoff example might call for softer Ls and Ms. Alternate singing with playing.

The small-scale details

In his memoirs, the Griller Quartet cellist Colin Hampton states that "the best way to help people learn something from memory is to have them write it out from memory first. If they can write it out, they'll know it."[20] This is a harder task than it seems. Even if someone could write down the time signatures, key signatures, note values, and pitches correctly, it would be a rare individual who could remember every tempo, dynamic, articulation, and expressive marking too.

This is why it's so important to return to the score regularly. Long after the notes of a composition are safely committed to memory, you should read through the score of your current pieces every day, both at and away from the cello, to make sure you're also memorizing the composer's expressive markings alongside the larger-scale elements of the composition.

Debussy, for example, always wrote many such markings into his scores, including detailed expressive directions in French. Following his directions as closely as possible is vital in a piece such as the Cello Sonata, which has marked timbral, tempo, and color contrasts in almost every measure. A composer such as Beethoven, by contrast, didn't write quite so many directions into the score, but his directions in all his compositions for strings, including the five cello sonatas—staccato marks of various types, sforzandi, bowings, his penchant for sudden dynamic changes—are deliberate and meaningful. Take time to notice markings in daily score preparation, and take care to follow them in practice.

Don't always start at the beginning

Memorizing short sections of a piece in random order is also a good idea, since trying to memorize straight through from beginning to end can result in the loss of concentration. For this reason, it is particularly helpful to work on passages from the end of the piece early in the practice session. You could try playing all the places the second theme appears, noticing where the key changes between sections of the piece. Sing the orchestral tutti sections that occur between cello solos to practice your pacing. Part of what causes memory lapses in concerts is not actually a problem with memorization but a problem with nerves in turn causing a lapse in attention to the formal and harmonic structure of a piece. Knowing exactly where you are in the score, in structural terms, will help you jump back in if you momentarily lose focus and miss a few notes.

Reflection away from the cello

Keep the piece you're working on ticking over in your head after you've finished practicing for the day. Go over it mentally while driving, doing chores, or drifting off to sleep. Think about where the melody and harmony are going as you play through it in your head, how it feels to make certain bowstrokes, and how your fingers will get from note to note. This reflective form of practice enables you to keep learning and memorizing even when you're not actively playing or studying the score. In his classic work on psychology, *Flow*, Mihaly Csikszentmihalyi notes that prisoners held in solitary confinement have managed to keep their physical skills at sporting and artistic activities by imagining themselves performing these activities in minute detail and with complete absorption.[21] This is memorization in its most heightened form.

Decreasing memorization anxiety

It goes without saying that the process of memorization is much easier for some individuals. For others, a memory slip in a concert features in their worst anxiety dreams. Often, it's not memorization itself that's the problem, but concentration. The fear of a memory lapse can itself be enough to disrupt concentration and spoil all the good memorization work that has taken place in the practice room. One bad experience of this nature can trigger a psychological complex about memorization from which it's not easy to recover. The best way to decrease this fear is to perform from memory as frequently as possible in low-stakes environments. This downplays the consequences—both positive and negative—of performing from memory and makes it more possible to treat performance as a rational extension of what you have achieved in practice.

Words and mnemonics

Another way to lessen anxiety about memory is to develop memory skills in extramusical ways. Memorization exercises are no longer popular in many educational philosophies because of a perception that they're boring and stifle creativity. But to make this complaint is to forget that every one of the creative arts requires us to memorize vast amounts of information, from brushstrokes to dance steps. Additionally, every aspect of how to function in society requires us to memorize vocabulary, names, faces, and rules, such as how to operate a car and drive it safely on the roads. Memorization doesn't have to be dull and fear-driven if you treat it as a fascinating exercise in understanding patterns. Because music mimics the rhythms and cadences of human speech, the practice of memorizing poetry may be an easier-to-remember first step in the process of improving your memorization of music. Just as the swinging rhythms of chanting multiplication tables, Latin cases, or prayers in religious rituals make them easy to remember with enough repetition, the key to successfully memorizing poetry is to look out for rhythmic, metrical, and rhyming patterns.

Because music has so much in common with word patterns—meter, rhythm, forms, articulations—it is no accident that there are so many mnemonic devices for memorization of musical concepts. From "Every Good Boy Deserves Fruit" and "All Cows Eat Grass" in the earliest stages of note-reading to made-up texts to famous melodies, mnemonics have memory-aiding power that may work faster than attempts to memorize untexted music. Orchestral musicians can easily recall both a historical fact and a melody in Schubert's Symphony no. 8 in B Minor, D. 759 ("Unfinished"), with the lyric attributed to the conductor Walter Damrosch: "This is the symphony that Schubert wrote and never finished." Part of self-teaching is to find devices, no matter how eccentric or silly, that help us learn.

First Steps in Memorizing Poetry

Start with an easy section of a poem, such as the last stanza of Tennyson's "Charge of the Light Brigade":

> When can their glory fade?
> O the wild charge they made!
> All the world wondered.
> Honor the charge they made,
> Honor the Light Brigade,
> Noble six hundred.

Notice the large-scale features: the AABAAB plan of the rhyme, the shape of the words that end each line. Next, notice smaller components, such as the number of syllables in the lines: the A lines have six, the B lines five. Notice the meter and rhythm of the lines. Notice the repetitive use of "charge they made" and "honor." Commit the first three lines to memory by repeating them a few times. Do the same with the next three. Notice the contrasting emotions between the two halves of the stanza: the first half dramatically grandiose ("glory," "wild," "all the world"), but the second calls us to respect the Light Brigade's sacrifice and legacy.

With practice, it is relatively easy to memorize stanzas of poetry and then to work your way up to memorizing entire poems. It will become increasingly easy to memorize more complicated forms, such Shakespeare's sonnets, which typically use the form of three quatrains and a couplet: ABAB CDCD EFEF GG. Start with one of the famous, familiar ones, such as Sonnet 18, "Shall I compare thee to a summer's day?"

HABIT NO. 8: SELF-RECORDING AND EVALUATION

The recording device—audio or video—is one of the most powerful self-teaching tools for practice and performance. Use the best equipment you can afford, but a mobile device with a video camera will work if you cannot access professional-quality equipment. The video camera should be as important in daily practice as the tuner, the metronome, or the drone.

You may find it embarrassing to listen to your own recordings because they reveal mistakes and inconsistencies that you might not have noticed at the time of playing. This is precisely the reason that you should self-evaluate using recordings every day in practice, not just for performances.

You don't have to video your entire practice session for recording to be useful; in fact, you'll learn more by making short videos. Start by thinking of a goal you want to accomplish in this session, such as performing a difficult run quickly and accurately.

Record the passage you'd like to improve. It doesn't matter if you fumble the notes, your fingers fall off the fingerboard, or your bow makes a scratching noise. The purpose of this exercise is to teach you how to play correctly. In other words, know how you want to sound, but acknowledge how you sound *right now*.

Constructive self-evaluation

Now watch and listen to the playback. Take some notes, using neutral, descriptive language, such as "I noticed that my left arm's tendency to sag in the neck position is making it more difficult for me to shift into the upper register, and my sound was smaller than I'd hoped because I played too close to the fingerboard without realizing I was doing it." Avoid negative, self-blaming language, such as "I totally messed up the shifts, and my sound was really bad." Self-castigation isn't productive. Instead, practice self-forgiveness. Say something affirming to yourself, like "I can do this. I'm already doing this. Now, let's figure out what happened, adjust a couple of things, and move forward."[22]

The next step is to start your practice session using the strategies detailed above. Work cross-laterally and creatively on experimental solutions to the problem. At the end of this work, make another video recording. Take note of the progress you made since the first video— and congratulate yourself. If there were still aspects of your performance you weren't pleased with—and there always are—write them down as goals for your next practice session.

Video public performances wherever possible, and watch them a few days later, when you've achieved some detachment after the initial, inevitable postmortem. Notice the things you tend to do in a concert that need adjustment. Notice what happened in your usual trouble spots, and devise some new strategies for working on them. Notice the things that went wrong that had never gone wrong before, and analyze what happened.

Be a hero in the practice room

Trying to be better in performance than you were in practice is a very common misjudgment. The surge of adrenaline you experience onstage often gives you a grandiose desire to "give it everything!" and you end up trying to make a bigger tone and bigger gestures than you've trained yourself to do. This causes extra tension in the body and manifests itself as a forced tone and rough phrasing.

A way around this is to practice your goal interpretation every time, even in the first stages of note-learning, even when repeating short excerpts. By doing this, you can predict more easily how a concert is going to go. If you want to play heroically in performance, you have to be a hero the rest of the time, too.

HABIT NO. 9: PERFORMING EVERY DAY

In the early stages of a career, high-stakes performances, such as competitions and degree recitals, may be rela-

tively infrequent, so it's important to seize opportunities for lower-profile performances. Playing in a café for tips, or in a nursing home for free, will give you a less nerve-wracking opportunity to notice how your body and mind react to adrenaline. From there, you can self-evaluate and adjust in your practice.

Seek teachers everywhere

You can also perform without seeking out formal performing opportunities. Ask family, friends, and colleagues to listen to you play every day, and take notes on how the performance went. Even when you're beyond the stage of having a regular teacher or mentor, ask colleagues for feedback. It can be painful to listen to their comments, but try to think of them as gifts that will help you improve. Take note of the suggestions, and practice them as if you had thought them up yourself. Let go of your pride: humility and willingness to try other people's ideas are hard lessons to learn, but valuable ones.

The imaginary audience

It's even possible to perform when you are the only person in the room. The act of performing music is as much a drama as any play, and musicians are the actors. Summon up an imaginary audience when you practice—play for them with the commitment you'd use in front of a real audience. If you approach this with enough imaginative visualizing, you should even be able to give yourself a rush of concert-level adrenaline. Conjuring up your own stage fright is a positive thing because it teaches you how to turn your nerves to your own advantage.

There is an appealing anecdote about the violinist Itzhak Perlman's preparation for his Carnegie Hall début.[23] Perlman, so the story goes, chose a date three months in advance of this all-important engagement for a practice run. When the day arrived, he put on concert clothes, waited in his kitchen as if it were backstage, then went out into the living room, which was his imaginary concert stage. He bowed, performed the first half for his imaginary audience, took an intermission, played the second half, and came back for his final bows.

Perlman was reportedly as nervous for this practice performance as he would have been for a real concert. When the date of the Carnegie Hall performance came about, however, he had far fewer nerves and performed

Part II

REPERTOIRE IN PRACTICE AND PERFORMANCE

Chapter Six

Harmonic Intonation in All Major and Minor Keys

Most of the canonical cello and string quartet repertoire comes from the era of diatonic music. Triadic constructions dominate such music, and yet tuning a triad can be complicated even for an advanced player. Every triadic chord on the cello requires us to negotiate around the open strings of the instrument, finding a suitable tuning for tones that do not correspond to open strings. Some keys, such as C, D, and E-flat, have historically been very popular in the cello and string ensemble literature because they work idiomatically with the construction of string instruments. Others, such as B major or E-flat minor, are less common.

Because this chapter deals with harmonic intonation, a large part of the examples will come from double- and triple-stopped passages in the solo cello literature, with a particular concentration on the six cello suites of J. S. Bach. Since string quartet playing is essential to the development of a strong sense of intonation, passages from the string quartet literature will also feature prominently.

These examples will address the problems and challenges of tuning harmonically in all keys, with suggestions for expressive solutions. However, it is important to remember that any concept of intonation is inexact and imperfect: one solution will not work on all occasions, because factors such as dynamics, tempo, tone quality (including vibrato), attack, and so on all affect intonation. In addition to this, factors such as modulation will affect the intonational concept of certain chords. There is also the matter of personal taste in the "negotiable" intervals, that is, dissonances and imperfect consonances: there is room for flexibility in many instances.

The key to all abbreviated directions is, as always, S = sharp; Fl. = flat; SR = use the sympathetic resonance of an open string; 0 = use the open string; (F) = play this note in tune with the previous F (or any other note that appears in parentheses).

C MAJOR

C, as the fundamental pitch of the cello, is one of the most common keys in cello and string music. In this example from the Allemande of Bach's Cello Suite no. 3 in C Major, BWV 1009, the cello begins a modulation from C major to G major by means of a tonic pedal that continues into a dominant pedal (fig. 6.1). All fingered Cs should be perfectly in tune with the open C-string to maximize the sympathetic resonance, as should all fingered Gs with the G-string. (Even if the C-string is tuned slightly sharp, as directed in chapter 3, the low pitch of the open string seems to compensate for the slight imperfection of the perfect fifth.) Fingered Ds and As should also be played exactly in tune with the open strings. The third of the C major triad, that is, E, should be slightly flat throughout this excerpt so that it is in tune both with the Cs and the Gs as the phrase moves towards modulation into G major. B, the third degree of the new G major triad, should also be slightly flat.

In measures 1–3 of the Sarabande from the same suite, the largely chordal first half of the movement also demands harmonic intonation (fig. 6.2). We can form a theory of how to tune it according to the principles of Roman numeral analysis. This example raises the issue of how to tune sevenths. In general, the seventh degree of the major-minor chord should be a little flat. This is because, in the rules of four-part harmony, the seventh degree of a V^7 chord resolves downwards in a V^7-I progression. In this part of the Sarabande, all Cs, Gs, Ds, and As that don't fall on open strings should be played exactly in tune with the open strings. Es and Bs are flat. Fs should be perfectly in tune with the C-string, meaning that they may sound slightly flat. B-flats should be perfectly in tune with the Fs, taking particular care in the second measure with the B-flat-F perfect fourth. The

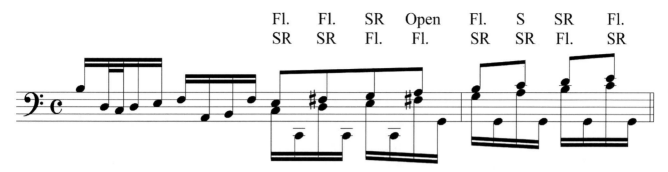

Figure 6.1.   Johann Sebastian Bach, Cello Suite no. 3 in C Major, BWV 1009, Allemande, mm. 6–7

markings in parentheses (the flat B in m. 1, the flat E in m. 3) may be played using linear intonation if desired, that is, not flat, because they do not fall on chordal notes, and therefore harmonic intonation is less important.

C MINOR

C minor is another very common key for the cello. In this passage from the first Gavotte in Bach's Suite no. 5 in C minor, Cs, Gs, and Ds must be in tune with the open strings (fig. 6.3). Fs should be in tune with the C-string. E-flats, B-flats, and A-flats should be somewhat sharp, with the possible exception of the second A-flat in measure 1, which can be played flatter to sound in tune with the open D-string. The second B-flat in the first measure can also be flatter so that it sounds in tune with F. (This also has the effect of better linear intonation—a concept not incompatible with the overall sense of harmonic intonation.) The B-natural in measure 2 may be played sharp, that is, with linear intonation, because it is the leading tone.

In the last five measures of the finale of Brahms's String Quartet in C Minor, op. 51, no. 1, the same principles apply (fig. 6.4). Here, however, the German sixth chord in the third measure may require some special treatment. Although the pitch classes of a German sixth are identical to those of a major-minor (V^7) chord, they do not need to be tuned the same way. One way to tune it is with flat A-flats and E-flats (relative to the open C-string), and a flat F-sharp. However, it can also be effective to experiment with different A-flat placements, moving the other notes around accordingly so the chord is "in tune with itself."

D-FLAT MAJOR

D-flat can be a troublesome key. The first decision the performer must make is the intonation of the D-flat. In a linear intonation context, it may be logical to place it somewhat flat, particularly since the leading tone, C, may take full advantage of the sympathetic resonance of the open string. Harmonic intonation, however, may demand

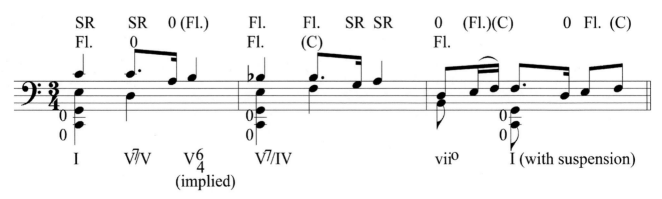

Figure 6.2.   Johann Sebastian Bach, Cello Suite no. 3 in C Major, BWV 1009, Sarabande, mm. 1–3

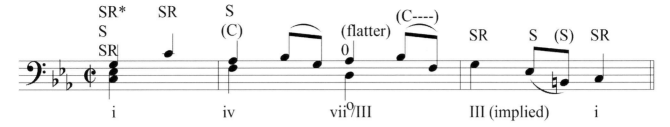

*If the cellist has tuned the A string down to G, as directed in some of the eighteenth-century manuscript sources, this note will be played on the open string.

Figure 6.3. Johann Sebastian Bach, Cello Suite no. 5 in C Minor, BWV 1011, Gavotte I, mm. 1–2

a different strategy. Sometimes, in keys where the tonic note has no sympathetic relation to an open string, it can be useful to place that note in relation to another degree of the triad that is more relatable to the open strings. In a D-flat major triad, therefore, it seems more intuitive to tune the F perfectly with the C-string, then tune the D-flat to the F. The D-flat will therefore be slightly sharp. If this seems artificial, consider that the dominant triad (A-flat) has C as its mediant note and will sound best if tuned to accommodate the C-string's resonance. The sharp D-flat method, although difficult in some ways, facilitates modulation to other keys, as in the following example from

the second movement of Beethoven's String Quartet op. 135 (fig. 6.5).

C-SHARP MINOR

C-sharp minor can also be problematic in terms of placing the tonic. In the following example from the seventh section of Beethoven's String Quartet in C-sharp Minor, op. 131, it may be desirable to place the C-sharp slightly flat, so that the minor third between C-sharp and the violins' open E-strings sounds in tune (fig. 6.6). All C-

Figure 6.4. Johannes Brahms, String Quartet in C Minor, op. 51, no. 1, movt. IV, mm. 244–48

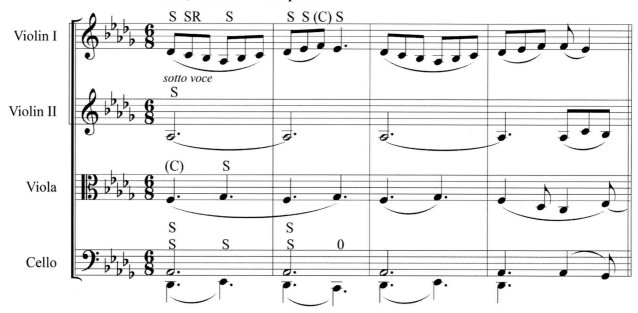

Figure 6.5.   **Ludwig van Beethoven, String Quartet in F Major, op. 135, movt. II, mm. 1–4**

sharps, F-sharps, and G-sharps, therefore, will be slightly flat. All As and Es will correspond to the open strings.

D MAJOR

D major is another of the most common keys in the cello—and strings—repertoire, partly because of its su-perior possibilities for resonance on all the instruments of the string family. This example from the third movement of Haydn's Cello Concerto in D Major, Hob. VIIb:2, is a fairly straightforward example of D major playing, utilizing the natural D, A, and E harmonics (fig. 6.7). The Es in measures 103 and 105 must be perfectly tuned to the A-string, though it's common to use a harmonic for the high E in measure 106 for the sake of resonance—and ease.

Figure 6.6.   **Ludwig van Beethoven, String Quartet in C-sharp Minor, op. 131, movt. VII, mm. 5–8**

Figure 6.7.   Franz Joseph Haydn, Cello Concerto in D Major, Hob. VIIb:2, movt. III, mm. 103–6

F-sharp, as the third degree of the D major triad, must be slightly flat. Gs must be perfectly tuned to the G-string.

More complicated is this example from the Sarabande of Bach's Suite no. 6 in D major, BWV 1012 (fig. 6.8). Here, the principles of music theory can help us establish a theory of intonation. It is clear that Ds, Gs, and As should be tuned to the open strings. F-sharp should be slightly flat. But what of the E and B in the second measure? In an E minor triad, it's possible to tune the E slightly flat so that the minor third between E and G is widened, and correspondingly put the B slightly flat so that the perfect fifth works. But many cellists prefer to tune the E directly against the E-natural harmonic that lies under the first finger in fourth position on the A-string, and tune the B against that. This may sound better linearly against the D sonority.

The C-sharp in the second measure is also a "negotiable" note: Since it's the leading tone, should we tune it linearly against the D, therefore making it slightly sharp? Or should we aim to have it an absolutely perfect fifth against the F-sharp-D double-stop that follows?

The vii° chord in the third measure is another that will respond well to experimentation. There are a variety of ways to tune a diminished triad. Simply trying to tune two minor thirds (C-sharp to E, E to G) may result in an out-of-tune chord. It may be more prudent to establish a desired tuning for the tritone formed by the two upper notes of the chord, then arrange the placement of the E to fit in with this.

D MINOR

D minor is just as common as D major in the string repertoire, if not more so. In this example from the opening of the first movement of Mozart's String Quartet in D Minor, K. 421, the F-naturals in the D minor triads will be played somewhat sharp (i.e., to sound in tune with the D and A) (fig. 6.9). In the second measure, the F in the viola part remains sharp, and the cello and second violin must tune their B-flat perfectly with this F to form a B-flat major triad. This B-flat is then passed to the violist in measure 3, and it stays sharp to correspond with the G and D in the cello and second violin parts. The violin's F should also be sharp, so as to be perfectly in tune with the B-flat. The imperfect authentic cadence that concludes this phrase has the added color of a ninth on top of the customary V⁷ chord. The tuning of this B-flat is negotiable. The first violinist may prefer to keep it sharp to be consistent with all the preceding B-flats. It could also conceivably work played flatter to outline the linear dissonance of the C-sharp/B-flat augmented second, and to emphasize the resolution onto the A on the last beat of the measure.

E-FLAT MAJOR

In spite of the challenges of tuning an E-flat major, it is a popular key in cello, chamber, and orchestral repertoire.

Figure 6.8.   Johann Sebastian Bach, Cello Suite no. 6 in D Major, BWV 1012, Sarabande, mm. 1–4

Figure 6.9.   Wolfgang Amadeus Mozart, String Quartet in D Minor, K. 421, movt. I, mm. 1–4

Bach's Suite no. 4, BWV 1010, Beethoven's Piano Trio in E-flat Major, op. 1, no. 1, String Quartet in E-flat Major, op. 74, and Symphony no. 3 in E-flat Major, op. 55 ("Eroica"), Schumann's Piano Quartet in E-flat Major, op. 47, and Piano Quintet in E-flat Major, op. 44, Mendelssohn's Octet in E-flat Major, op. 20, and Shostakovich's Cello Concerto no. 1 in E-flat Major, op. 107, are just a handful of the great compositions for cello in this key. The easiest way to tune an E-flat is to pitch it slightly sharp against the open G-string (fig. 6.10). (Add a B-flat that is perfectly in tune with E-flat to form the triad.)

One of the best exercises for harmonic intonation in the key of E-flat is Popper's Étude no. 9 from his *High School of Cello Playing* op. 73 (fig. 6.11). The first phrase alone teaches many important lessons in the art of intonation.

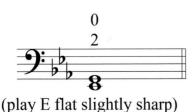

(play E flat slightly sharp)

Figure 6.10.   Tuning an E-flat against the open G-string

Using this system of harmonic intonation, all E-flats and B-flats should be slightly sharp so that they are in tune with the open G-string. All A-flats should also be slightly sharp, partly because they need to sound in tune with the E-flats and partly because when the A-flat is played with a C that is tuned to the open C-string, it will need to be slightly sharp because A-flat and C form a major third, and major thirds need to be "narrow." Therefore, all Fs must be in tune with the Cs so they match the A-flats. This works because F and A-flat form a minor third, and minor thirds need to be "wide."

J. S. Bach's Cello Suite no. 4 in E-flat Major, BWV 1010, presents many challenges, not least of which is playing long and physically taxing movements in tune (fig. 6.12). The Popper étude above is a good preparatory exercise for the surprisingly hard skill of consistently hitting E-flat in tune. Cultivating this intuitive sense of E-flat placement is very helpful in the Sarabande and the second Bourrée of the suite. In this example from the Bourrée, the most difficult aspect of intonation is keeping the perfect fifths in tune. Though it may appear that almost every note must be played counterintuitively sharp, this practice is really only working around the sympathetic resonances of the open strings to maximize the resonance of the stopped notes.

Andante sostenuto

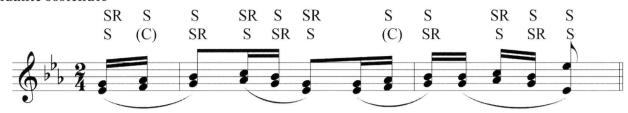

Figure 6.11.   David Popper, *High School of Cello Playing* op. 79, no. 9, mm. 1–2

The different movements demand different intonational concepts. Bach's writing in the Prelude is linear rather than chordal, but it is still appropriate to use harmonic rather than linear intonation, because the broken chords that compose the melodic line give a more vertical than horizontal impression (fig. 6.13).

The more melodic linear movements may call for an entirely different placement of the E-flat, however. In the Allemande, by contrast with the Prelude, the writing is almost exclusively linear and highly melodic, with only one chord at the very end (fig. 6.14). Since linear rather than harmonic intonation is indicated, it may be better to find a nonsharp or even slightly *flat* E-flat, so that we may take advantage of the open D-string as a (sharp) leading tone. It is up to the player to decide whether having a differently tuned tonic for the Prelude will sound jarring to the audience's ear, or whether the change is worth it for the increased ease of playing and the leading tone-tonic relation of the E-flat to the open D-string.

In string ensemble music in the key of E-flat, the choices for E-flat placement are usually clearer. In the opening measures of Beethoven's String Quartet in E-flat Major, op. 74, the group intonation of the individual chords is more important than the linear properties of the cello's descending phrase (fig. 6.15). The entire opening Adagio goes through unexpected and chromatic harmonic changes, veering almost immediately away from the E-flat major triads of the first and third measures and creating a sense of great anticipation and longing for an

E-flat resolution that does not arrive until the beginning of the Allegro section at measure 25.

The first chord should feature a sharp E-flat for the first violin and cello, a G in tune with the G-string for the second violin, and a sharp B-flat for the viola. This same tuning applies to the second chord, but the cello now has a seventh, a D-flat. The seventh degree of a major-minor seventh chord is generally played slightly flat. Because the E-flat will probably be considerably sharp, there is no need for the D-flat to be extremely flat. However, if we were to hear the cello part played alone using this kind of intonation, the line in the first measure would sound out of tune by the principles of linear intonation. It will not sound that way when the other three instruments are playing, however: this is one of the sacrifices we must make for the group's overall intonation and blend of sounds.

E-FLAT MINOR

E-flat minor is a very rare key for any type of instrumentation, and particularly for strings, perhaps because of the cumbersome six-sharp key signature or the lack of correspondences with the open strings. The only major string compositions in E-flat minor are Shostakovich's String Quartet no. 15 in E-flat Minor, op. 144, where the muted resonance of the key on the instruments is perfect for the hushed, eerie mood of much of the writing, and Tchaikovsky's String Quartet op. 30.

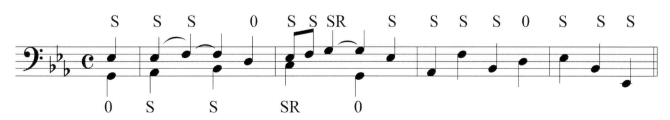

Figure 6.12.   Johann Sebastian Bach, Cello Suite no. 4 in E-flat Major, BWV 1010, Bourrée II, mm. 1–4

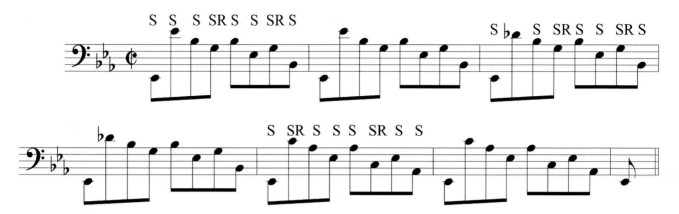

Figure 6.13. Johann Sebastian Bach, Cello Suite no. 4 in E-flat Major, BWV 1010, Prelude, mm. 1-6

Figure 6.14. Johann Sebastian Bach, Cello Suite no. 4 in E-flat Major, BWV 1010, Allemande, mm. 1–2

Figure 6.15. Ludwig van Beethoven, String Quartet in E-flat Major, op. 74, movt. I, mm. 1–4

In E-flat minor, the tuning of E-flat will be significantly different from that of E-flat major, where it should be sharp in order to correspond with the open G. There is no need to play the tonic note sharp in E-flat minor. In fact, there is no obvious indication of where to put the E-flat at all, since none of the notes of the E-flat-natural minor scale corresponds to an open string. In the example below, from the third movement of Tchaikovsky's opus 30, the placement of the E-flat is at the players' discretion (fig. 6.16).

When making this decision, however, consider also the relation of the E-flat to the modulations in the piece. In this Tchaikovsky movement, there are episodes in several far-flung keys, such as B major. The common tones between E-flat minor and B major will be spelled enharmonically, that is, the E-flat of E-flat minor will

Figure 6.16. Pyotr Ilich Tchaikovsky, String Quartet in E-flat Minor, op. 30, movt. III, mm. 25–29

Figure 6.17. François Francoeur, Cello Sonata in E Major, movt. II, mm. 3–4

correspond with the D-sharp that is part of the B major triad. But does it? The players must decide whether these enharmonic notes should have the same intonation. Does the arrival of a new key signal a different color altogether, or should the transition be as intonationally seamless as possible?

E MAJOR

This is a relatively rare key for cello music in comparison with other stringed instruments; this may be because of the cello's lack of an E-string. Because of the principles of the overtone series, however, E major can still utilize sympathetic resonance from the open A-string. The most commonly played piece for cello in E major that features harmonic intonation is François Francoeur's Cello Sonata (fig. 6.17). In this section from the second movement, the dominant-tonic harmonic motion provides an excellent exercise in harmonic intonation in E major. The E, naturally, should be as perfectly in tune with the A-string as possible. B should be perfectly in tune with E, and G-sharp should be slightly flat. The F-sharp should be perfectly in tune with the B, and the D-sharp should be slightly flat.

Even though pieces in E major are rare, the E major triad is often heard as the dominant function in the more common key of A major. This example from the second movement of Haydn's Cello Concerto in D Major is a good example of how to tune a chain of thirds in E major (fig. 6.18). The E should be in tune with the E-strings of the orchestral violin section, hence the direction for sympathetic resonance.

The string quartet repertoire has slightly more examples of E major, such as Schubert's String Quartet in E Major, D. 353, and the last movement of Smetana's String Quartet no. 1 in E Minor, JB 1:105 ("From My Life"). This example from the Smetana shows how the brilliant resonance from the second violinist's open E-string guides the principles of the harmonic intonation (fig. 6.19). The cellist should of course play the G-sharps slightly flat.

E MINOR

There are a number of ways to find the E of E minor. In music where the cello plays alone, there is no open E-string, and there are times when it will seem natural to play the E flatter than an "E-string E." Because of the necessity of tuning the E minor triad against the open G-string in this example from the opening of Elgar's Cello Concerto in E Minor, op. 85, the E will be a "G-string E" and therefore rather flatter than an "E-major E" (fig. 6.20). Later in the first movement, however, it will be desirable to use linear rather than harmonic intonation and to shift the tuning of the E to that of the violin E-string, as in the passage in figure 6.21.

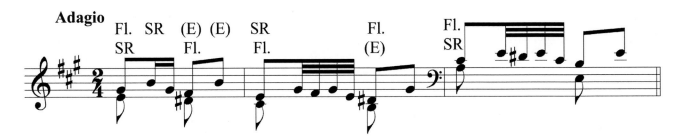

Figure 6.18. Franz Joseph Haydn, Cello Concerto in D Major, Hob. VIIb:2, movt. II, mm. 24–26

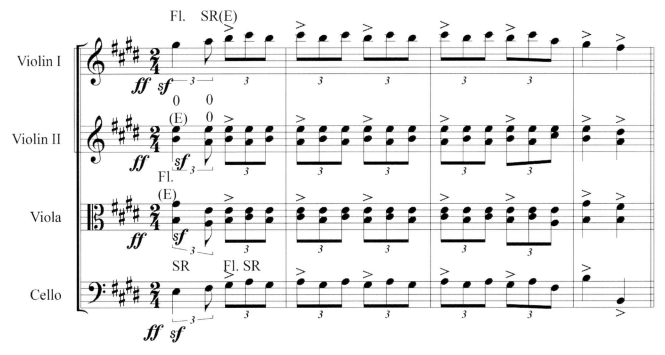

Figure 6.19. Bedřich Smetana, String Quartet in E Minor, JB 1:105 ("From My Life"), movt. IV, mm. 1–4

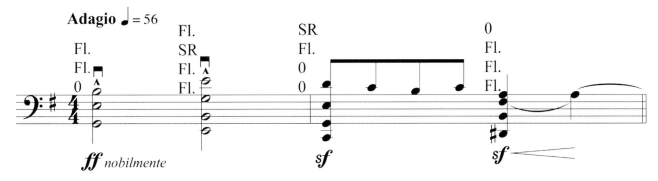

Figure 6.20. Edward Elgar, Cello Concerto in E Minor, op. 85, movt. I, mm. 1–2

Figure 6.21. Edward Elgar, Cello Concerto in E Minor, op. 85, movt. I, mm. 27–28

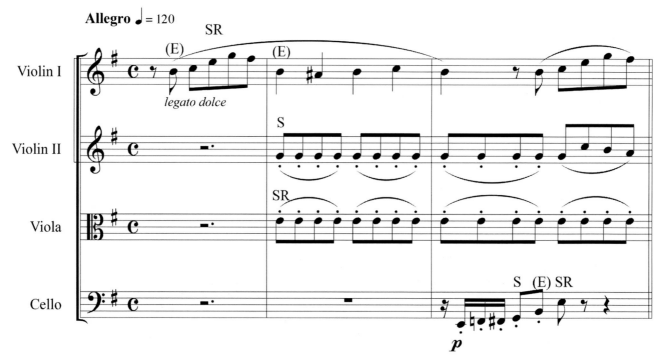

Figure 6.22.   Giuseppe Verdi, String Quartet in E Minor, movt. I, mm. 10–11

In E minor passages in quartet music, the players must work around the conflict between the open E- and G-strings. If, for example, the first violinist plays an open E-string and the second violinist plays an open G, the resulting major thirteenth will not sound particularly well in tune. In most circumstances, it will be more prudent to tune the E minor triad to the violins' E- string, as in this example from Verdi's String Quartet in E Minor (fig. 6.22). In this case, the second violinist should play the G slightly sharper than a "G-string G."

F MAJOR

It may come as a surprise to beginning chamber music players that F major is one of the most problematic triads to tune. It's difficult because there is more than one possibility for finding the F. One way is to tune it to the open A-string. The other is to tune it to the open C-string. But even if the cello's C-string is tuned as sharp as is bearably possible, there will still be a discrepancy between an "A-string F" (a sharper F) and a "C-string F" (a flatter

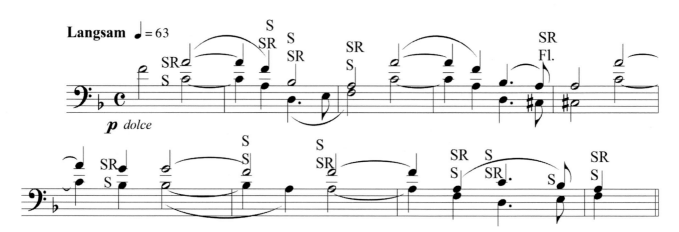

Figure 6.23.   Robert Schumann, Cello Concerto in A Minor, op. 129, movt. II, mm. 18–26

F). In the majority of circumstances, the F major triad works best with the "A-string F," but the key in general is so troublesome, particularly when shifting between tonic and dominant, that it is worth examining several examples of F major that respond to differing procedures.

In this example from the second movement of Schumann's Cello Concerto in A Minor, op. 129, the cello plays a double-stopped passage in F major that works well with an "A-string F," not least because the overall key of the concerto is A minor (fig. 6.23). (A caution: normally when playing a solo concerto with an orchestra, certain concessions to wind and brass intonation are necessary because of the instruments' different intonation systems and because the players will not be able to hear the cello soloist during their solos. However, in this one instance, the accompaniment to the double-stopped passage is composed exclusively for strings, apart from a short horn solo at the beginning. The possibilities for

Figure 6.24. **Maurice Ravel, String Quartet in F Major, movt. I, mm. 1–4**

harmonic intonation are therefore much more flexible.) Most F major string quartet movements will also use an "A-string F," at least at the beginning of the movement. In this example from the first movement of Ravel's String Quartet in F Major, an "A-string F" system works well (fig. 6.24).

There is an exception to every rule. In some cases, a preponderance of Cs in the harmonic voicing of an F major passage may mean that it simply works better to tune the F to the C-string. An example of a passage in F major that responds better to a "C-string F" can be found in the first movement of Beethoven's String Quartet op. 59, no. 1 (fig. 6.25). Although the key signature is F major, there is no root-position F major triad until measure 19. The opening broadly hints at F major without actually confirming it in the cello part, but the C-heavy line sounds most resonant when the Cs are tuned exactly with the C-string.

The usefulness of this strategy is revealed between measures 13 and 20, where the voicing of the longed-for perfect authentic cadence demands an open C from the cello (fig. 6.26). If the ensemble had been using "A-string Fs," this progression would sound badly out of tune. As it is, the awkwardness of tuning F to the C-string demands that the cellist and violist tune their open C-strings even sharper than usual, particularly if the second violinist uses an open A-string on the downbeat of measure 19. The notorious difficulty of tuning this movement means that the players must, at times, sacrifice the tuning of certain notes and chords to make others work.

F MINOR

The choice of F tuning is simpler in F minor than in F major. Because A-natural is not part of the key signature, there is no need to tune F to the A-string; the F should be a "C-string F." In the first movement of Mendelssohn's String Quartet in F Minor, op. 80, the opening F in the cello part should sound quite flat so that it is a perfectly tuned fifth with the viola's open C-string (fig. 6.27).

F-SHARP MINOR AND F-SHARP MAJOR

These two parallel modes are grouped together because F-sharp major seldom exists independently of F-sharp minor. Indeed, F-sharp major is a very rare home key in the string repertoire, and its enharmonic, G-flat major, is almost unknown outside of a handful of orchestral pieces. (The second movement of Brahms's Cello Sonata in F Major, op. 99, is in F-sharp major, but the piano, rather than the principles of harmonic intonation, dictates the tuning of the F-sharp tonic and tonic triad, so it is not relevant to this discussion.)

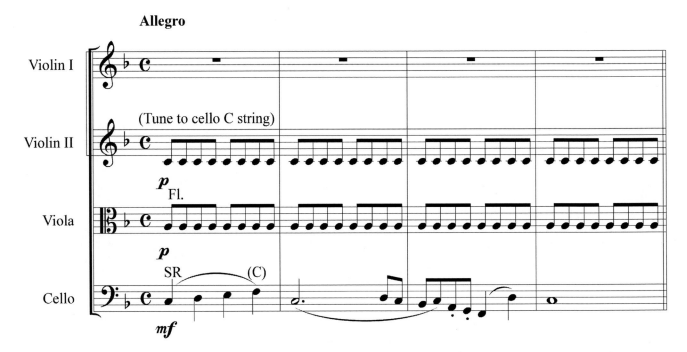

Figure 6.25. Ludwig van Beethoven, String Quartet in F Major, op. 59, no. 1 ("Razumovsky"), movt. I, mm. 1–4

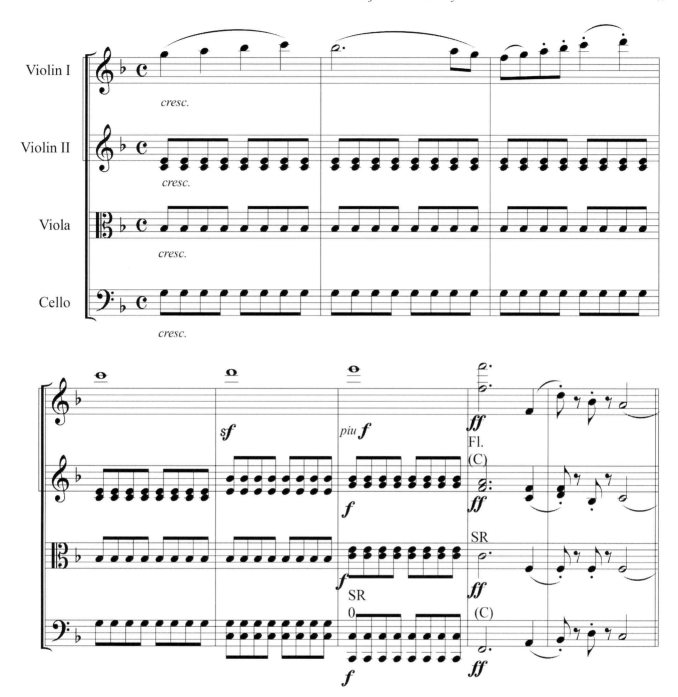

Figure 6.26.   Ludwig van Beethoven, String Quartet in F Major, op. 59, no. 1 ("Razumovsky"), movt. I, mm. 13–20

In the F-sharp minor triad, the F-sharp should be in tune with the open A-string and therefore sound slightly flat. In this example from Haydn's String Quartet in F-sharp Minor, op. 50, no. 4, the players can achieve optimal resonance by tuning Es, As, and Ds exactly with the open strings and by adjusting F-sharps and C-sharps to sound slightly flat against the open strings (fig. 6.28).

F-sharp major is usually only found in passing in the string quartet repertoire. Sometimes it appears in development sections, where composers often modulate to or tonicize keys that are distantly related to the home key. On other occasions, it appears at the end of an F-sharp minor movement in the form of a Picardy third, as in the first movement of Shostakovich's String Quartet no. 7

Allegro vivace assai

Figure 6.27.   Felix Mendelssohn, String Quartet in F Minor, op. 80, movt. I, mm. 1–9

in F-sharp Minor, op.108. Haydn's String Quartet in F-sharp Minor, op. 50, no. 4, contains significant sections in F-sharp major, including the coda to the first movement and the Minuet part of the Minuet and Trio. When F-sharp major appears, the context will usually give some clue as to the tuning of the F-sharp. In this example from the Haydn, the F-sharp major Minuet gives way to the F-sharp minor Trio in the example below (fig. 6.29), and

the players must decide whether to use the same F-sharp for both major and minor modes or to exaggerate the coloristic contrast between modes by changing the F-sharp. Most recordings of this work appear to keep the same F-sharp for both modes, however.

An F-sharp major interlude in Hugo Wolf's *Italian Serenade* proceeds directly into another type of abrupt key change (fig. 6.30). In this example, the placement of

Figure 6.28.   Franz Joseph Haydn, String Quartet in F-sharp Minor, op. 50, no. 4, movt. I, mm. 1–8

the F-sharp (and, by extension, the C-sharp and A-sharp) is determined by the fact that it functions as the mediant note of the D major triad in the following section. Because fingered Ds are almost always tuned exactly with the open D-string, this means the F-sharp will need to be slightly flat so that the second violinist doesn't need to change the pitch over the double barline into a D major triad.

G MAJOR

Like C major, G major can sound particularly open and resonant on string instruments because its key signature includes open-string correspondences with every one of the strings on the cello and violin. (Essentially, G major is to the violin what C major is to the cello.) The root and fifth of the triad can correspond exactly with the open

Figure 6.29. Franz Joseph Haydn, String Quartet in F-sharp Minor, op. 50, no. 4, movt. III, mm. 36–42

strings, and the B can sit slightly flat. Cellists often find this G major passage from the first movement of Haydn's Cello Concerto in C Major, Hob. VIIb:1, difficult to tune (fig. 6.31); it may help to listen deliberately for the harmonic intonation of the thirds.

The most famous cello composition in G major is, of course, Bach's Cello Suite no. 1 in G Major, BWV 1007. The Allemande, Courante, Menuets, and Gigue will mostly work best with linear intonation, but the Prelude and Sarabande respond well to harmonic intonation. Though the Prelude's harmonies appear in linear form, the concept of the piece is vertical rather than horizontal (similar to the Prelude from the Cello Suite no. 4 in E-flat Major, BWV 1010, in fact), so harmonic intonation may be preferable (fig. 6.32). The Sarabande's partially chordal texture more clearly demands harmonic intonation (fig. 6.33). In this example, a pedal G remains constant while the harmony changes above it.

Many quartet compositions also take advantage of the felicitous resonance of G major. This excerpt from Mozart's String Quartet in G Major, K. 387, illustrates a fairly typical Classical chord progression (fig. 6.34). The

Figure 6.30. Hugo Wolf, *Italian Serenade*, mm. 118–30

Figure 6.31. Franz Joseph Haydn, Cello Concerto in D Major, Hob. VIIb:1, movt. I, mm. 40–41

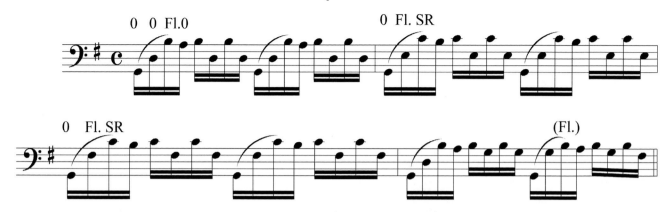

Figure 6.32.   Johann Sebastian Bach, Cello Suite no. 1 in G Major, BWV 1007, Prelude, mm. 1–4

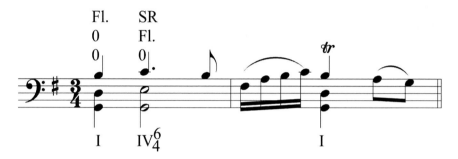

Figure 6.33.   Johann Sebastian Bach, Cello Suite no. 1 in G Major, BWV 1007, Sarabande, mm. 1–2

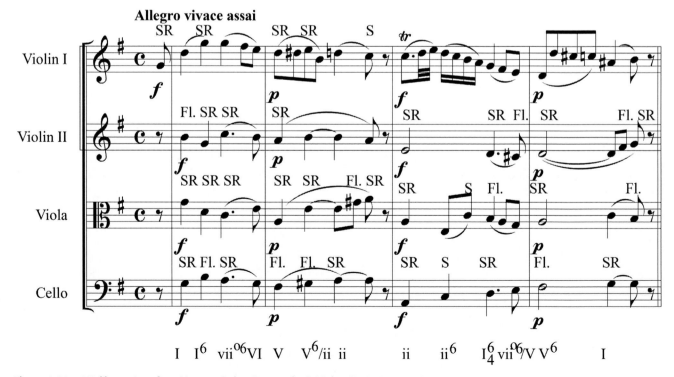

Figure 6.34.   Wolfgang Amadeus Mozart, String Quartet in G Major, K. 387, movt. I, mm. 1–4

preponderance of first inversion chords means that the cellist will have to adjust the pitches of the various thirds flat or sharp, depending on whether the chord is major or minor. The first violinist will probably elect to use linear intonation for measures 3 and 4; the others should adjust their intonation accordingly.

G MINOR

Though G minor utilizes the sympathetic resonances of all the open strings too, it has less of the brightness of G ma-

jor. The slow movement from Schubert's String Quartet in D Minor, D. 810 ("Death and the Maiden"), uses its somber, serious color in a set of variations on the section from the original *Lied* that is sung by the character of Death: "Give me your hand, you beautiful, sweet creature! I am a friend, and do not come to punish" (fig. 6.35).

The intonation of the above theme is straightforward enough: Cs, Gs, Ds, and As in tune with the open strings; sharp B-flats and E-flats. Intonation in the second variation, however, can be more flexible (fig. 6.36). Here, the cellist has the melodic solo, and the other three instruments take

Figure 6.35.   Franz Schubert, String Quartet in D Minor, D. 810 ("Death and the Maiden"), movt. II, mm. 1–8

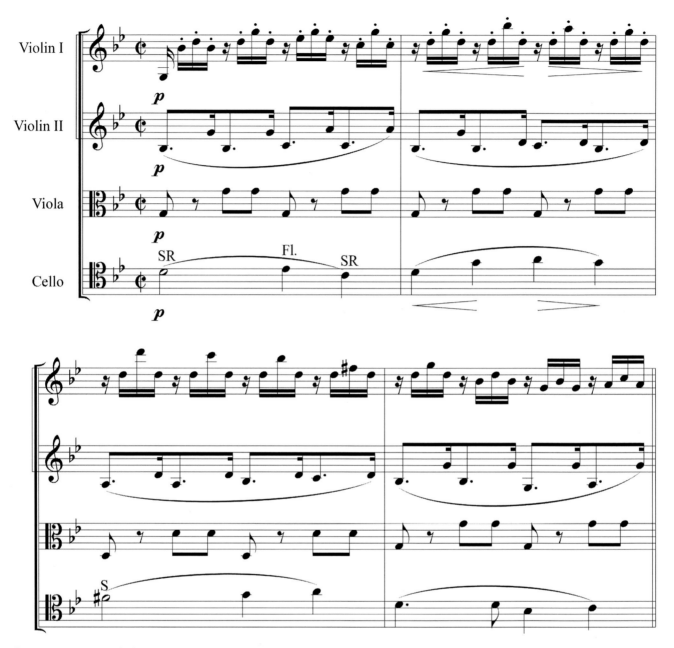

Figure 6.36.   Franz Schubert, String Quartet in D Minor, D. 810 ("Death and the Maiden"), movt. II, mm. 49–52

over the harmonic accompaniment. Under normal circumstances, the cello's bassline "leads" the intonation from the bottom, but here the viola functions as the bassline, so the cello has more freedom to exercise linear intonation.

The violinists and violist should still abide by the principles of harmonic intonation, but the voicing of the harmonies means that there is no conflict of intonation if the cellist wants to play a flat E-flat or a sharp F-sharp. No system of intonation should be a rigid orthodoxy. It's better to exercise flexibility and to look for the most expressive solution to any interpretative challenge.

A-FLAT MAJOR

The most straightforward solution for tuning the A-flat major triad is to pitch A-flat and E-flat somewhat sharp against the open C-string. This works well when the principal key is A-flat major, as in the third movement of Smetana's String Quartet no. 1 (fig. 6.37).

The challenge of A-flat major is dealing with modulations to and from other keys. For example, this passage from measures 58 through 69 in the fourth movement of Dvořák's String Quartet in F Major ("American"), op.

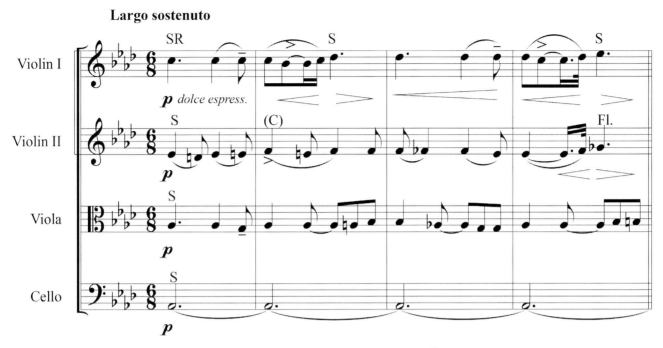

Figure 6.37. Bedřich Smetana, String Quartet no. 1 in E Minor, JB 1:105 ("From My Life"), movt. III, mm. 7–10

96, modulates from F major to A-flat major by way of a C pivot (fig. 6.38). A potential problem is that the F major triad uses an "A-string F" rather than an F that is in tune with the C-string. Since an open C resonance is necessary for the A-flat triad, the players may wish to make the Cs from measure 62 onwards slightly flatter in preparation for the arrival in A-flat major. Leaving A-flat major is considerably easier, because the next key Dvořák goes into is C minor (m. 77), which of course uses the same C-string intonation (fig. 6.39).

A-FLAT MINOR/G-SHARP MINOR

A-flat minor and G-sharp minor usually only appear in passing, often as tonicizations of distant keys in sonata-form-development sections. One example that goes through both keys is an A-flat minor passage that morphs into G-sharp minor at the end of the development in the first movement of the Dvořák Cello Concerto (mm. 224–40 and beyond) (fig. 6.40). Linear intonation works best for the first part of this theme where the cello has the melodic role; when the orchestral woodwind takes over the melody at measure 240, the cello's passage-work demands harmonic intonation. The intonation of the orchestral woodwind accompaniment, particularly of the flutes and oboes, will determine the tuning of the G-sharp; however, the harmony will dictate the placement of the mediant notes of triads.

Sometimes A-flat minor appears in an A-flat major movement as its parallel minor. In this passage from measures 21–27 of the second movement of Beethoven's String Quartet in E-flat Major, op. 74, the principal key of A-flat major switches abruptly in measure 23 to the parallel minor mode (fig. 6.41). The groups in most recordings maintain the same A-flat between A-flat major and A-flat minor, but a small minority take a new, flatter A-flat in measure 23 (starting from the cello's upper A-flat on beat 2) to create a darker, more muted color. This can be an interesting discussion and experiment to conduct in rehearsal.

A MAJOR

With its sympathetic resonances from A-strings and violin E-strings, A major is one of the brighter keys in the spectrum. In a string quartet context, this makes for straightforward tuning, with the C-sharp of the triad slightly flat, as in this example from the opening measures of the second movement of Mozart's String Quartet in D Major, K. 575 (fig. 6.42).

There is not much harmonically tuned A major to be found in the solo cello repertoire, except where it functions as the dominant of D, in the Bach D minor and D major suites, for example, and in Haydn's Cello Concerto in D Major (whose second movement is in A major). There are many possibilities for harmonic intonation in the Haydn,

Figure 6.38.   Antonín Dvořák, String Quartet in F Major ("American"), op. 96, movt. IV, mm. 58–69

including this A major double-stopped passage from the first movement (fig. 6.43). The intonation of harmonically played minor sevenths depends on context: in a V^7 chord, for example, the seventh will be played lower because in the rules of voice-leading, and it resolves downwards; this 4-3 movement sounds particularly good when the seventh is lower. Here, however, the minor seventh is a

suspensional rather than dominant-functional dissonance, so it is not necessary to make the top note lower. Rather, it is easiest to enjoy the clash of the appoggiatura and the subsequent resolution into a major or minor sixth. The top note of the minor seventh, therefore, uses general A major intonation; the minor sixth is slightly widened, and the major sixths are slightly narrowed.

Figure 6.39.   Antonín Dvořák, String Quartet in F Major ("American"), op. 96, movt. IV, mm. 69–78

A MINOR

Like A major, the minor mode utilizes a great deal of open-string resonance. A minor is a slightly special case, in that the third of the minor triad is C. This raises the A-string vs. C-string conflict. Usually in a minor triad, the third should be sharpened; even when the C-string is tuned sharp, however, it will not sound sharp against the open A-string. There are various solutions: one could

be to tune the C-string extra sharp, but if the movement modulates to C, the relative major, this will cause its own set of tuning problems. It may be more satisfactory to play fingered Cs slightly sharper than the C-string, even at the expense of maximal sympathetic resonance, as in this example from the third movement of Brahms's String Quartet in A Minor, op. 51, no. 2 (fig. 6.44).

Sometimes the open C-string cannot be avoided, as in this passage from the same Brahms movement, where

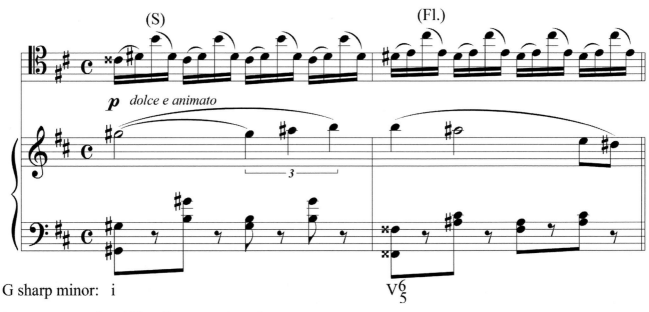

Figure 6.40.   Antonín Dvořák, Cello Concerto in B Minor, op. 104, movt. I, mm. 240–41

repeated open Cs in the cello cause tuning problems (fig. 6.45). In this case, all fingered As should be as flat as is bearable. After the last open C-string, normal A minor tuning should resume.

B-FLAT MAJOR

Solo cello compositions in B-flat are relatively rare; the main example is the Boccherini–Grützmacher Cello Concerto in B-flat. Other than that, B-flat functions more often as the dominant triad in E-flat movements, such as in the second halves of the dance movements in Bach's Cello Suite no. 4. The difficulty of the key does, however, make it a favorite of étude composers. Piatti's legendarily difficult Caprice no. 3 in B-flat is an exercise in double-stopping, and therefore harmonic intonation, in B-flat (fig. 6.46). B-flats and Fs should be played sharp so that they're in tune with the D-string.

Figure 6.41.   Ludwig van Beethoven, String Quartet in E-flat Major, op. 74, movt. II, mm. 21–27

Figure 6.42.   Wolfgang Amadeus Mozart, String Quartet in D Major, K. 575, movt. II, mm. 1–4

Figure 6.43.   Franz Joseph Haydn, Cello Concerto in D Major, Hob. VIIb:2, movt. I, mm. 71–72

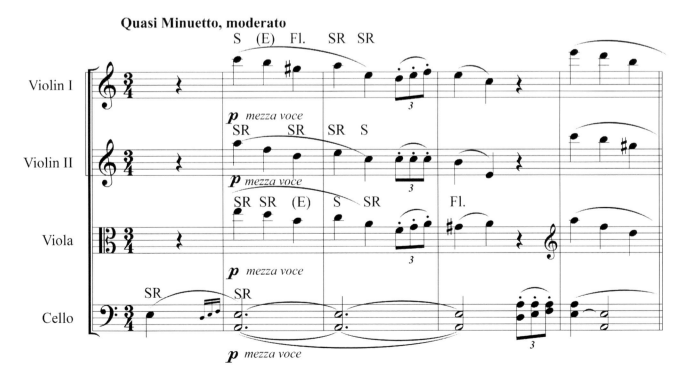

Figure 6.44.   Johannes Brahms, String Quartet in A Minor, op. 51, no. 2, movt. III, mm. 1–4

Figure 6.45.   Johannes Brahms, String Quartet in A Minor, op. 51, no. 2, movt. III, mm. 123–33

Figure 6.46.   Alfredo Piatti, *12 Caprices* op. 25, no. 3, mm. 1–8

The string quartet repertoire has several compositions in B-flat major, such as Mozart's String Quartet in B-flat Major, K. 458 ("Hunt"), Beethoven's String Quartet in B-flat Major, op. 130, and Brahms's String Quartet in B-flat Major, op. 67, and also individual movements, such as the second movement of Beethoven's String Quartet in F Major, op. 59, no. 1 (fig. 6.47). Here, the occasionally linear texture allows for a certain flexibility in intonation; for example, the G-flat and E-natural that occur seven and six measures before the end can sound closer to the F, further accentuating the functional "pull" of the dominant.

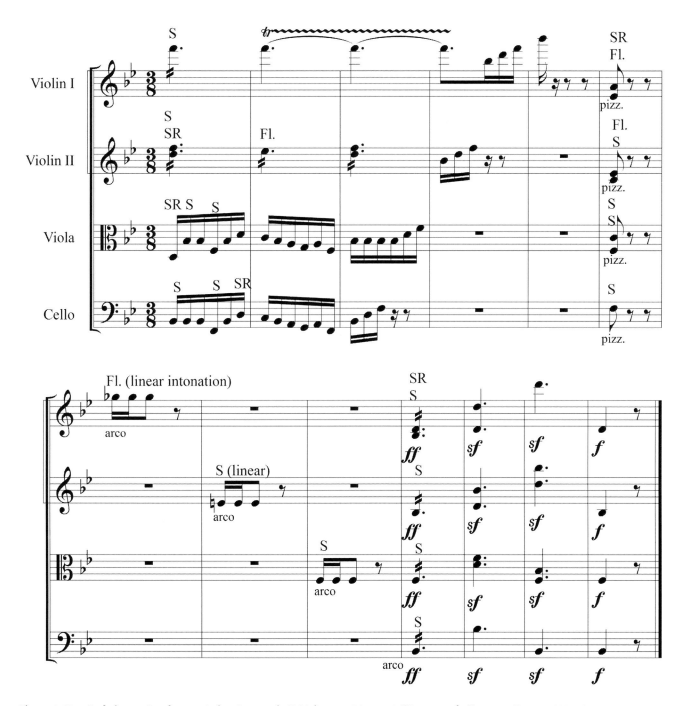

Figure 6.47. Ludwig van Beethoven, String Quartet in F Major, op. 59, no. 1 ("Razumovsky"), movt. II, mm. 464–76

B-FLAT MINOR

B-flat minor is another of the rarest keys in the cello and string repertoire. The best-known quartet movement in B-flat minor is the slow movement of Samuel Barber's String Quartet op. 11, which is more commonly played in Barber's own string orchestra arrangement, *Adagio for Strings*. Though firmly within the realms of extended

diatonicism, it is not, however, firmly in B-flat minor at any point, and therefore is not the best example of how to tune in this key.

B-flat minor can usually be found as the parallel minor in a B-flat major piece, as in this example from the last movement of Brahms's String Quartet in B-flat Major, op. 67 (fig. 6.48). The players must choose whether to keep the "D-string B-flat" of the B-flat major variations

Figure 6.48.   Johannes Brahms, String Quartet in B-flat Major, op. 67, movt. IV, mm. 52–58

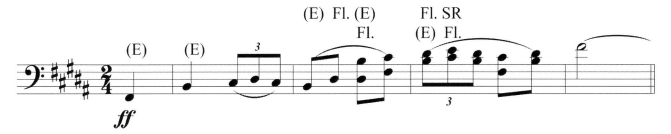

Figure 6.49. Antonín Dvořák, Cello Concerto in B Minor, op. 104, movt. III, mm. 426–29

Figure 6.50. Antonín Dvořák, Cello Concerto in B Minor, op. 104, movt. I, mm. 261–62

or to flatten the B-flat to alter the color. If the B-flat goes flatter, it should match a "C-string F," as shown.

B MAJOR

B major is another extremely rare key in cello music, probably because the B major scale contains no sympathetic resonances with the cello's open strings. B major triads function chiefly as the dominant in E major movements or as the parallel major in B minor movements. Dvořák's Cello Concerto in B Minor, op. 104, contains several B major sections, with both first and third movements ending in B major. The presence of E in the B major scale suggests that the B should be perfectly in tune with a violin E-string, but like many examples of tonic tuning on the cello, this is open to debate. This example of double-stops from the third movement illustrates the tuning of the tonic and dominant chords (fig. 6.49).

B MINOR

Just as the parallel majors and minors of E-flat, E, F, and B-flat sometimes require different tonic tunings between modes, B major and B minor may also need two differ-

ent Bs. In order to tune a B minor triad perfectly with the open D-string, the Bs and F-sharps will need to be slightly flat. In this example from the first movement of the Dvořák, the sympathetic resonances of the D- and G-strings propel the intonation (fig. 6.50).

SUMMARY OF HARMONIC INTONATION IN ALL MAJOR AND MINOR KEYS

- When tuning the tonic triad in any key, consider which—if any—notes of the triad correspond with the open strings of the cello or the other stringed instruments. Evaluate the best placement of the tonic note.
- Sometimes there will be more than one possibility for tuning the tonic note. When this is the case, examine the harmonic context of the triad. Where does it modulate to? How can intonation help achieve a seamless modulation?
- Harmonic intonation will not be appropriate for every musical context. Carefully evaluate all options and find a consensus on what sounds best.
- As in all areas of music-making, experimentation and discussion with colleagues are the keys to forming a convincing interpretation. The guidelines for harmonic intonation are just that—guidelines, not immutable rules. The art of tuning is a lifelong challenge.

Chapter Seven

Composing Your Own Études

Good cellists are made, not born. No one is instantly able to play Tchaikovsky's *Variations on a Rococo Theme* op. 33 or Dvořák's Cello Concerto op. 104 without a great deal of practice, and any cellist will need to work on problematic passages in the repertoire many times before being able to perform them confidently.

All the great cello concertos contain virtuoso sections that showcase a particular skill—double-stops, rapid dashing all over the instrument, string-crossing passages in a high position, off-the-string bowstrokes—that we need to learn to play accurately, expressively, and reliably. But mastering just one isolated skill—octaves in the left hand or uncontrolled spiccato in the right—does no good if the actions of the other hand are not an integrated part of it. This is why practicing uncontrolled spiccato on an open string won't help with the frantic runs in the second movement of Elgar's Cello Concerto op. 85, and practicing the runs without the bow won't accomplish anything either. The two must be practiced together in coordination for anything to be accomplished.

The second movement of Elgar's Cello Concerto is not, of course, the place to start learning to play un-controlled spiccato for the first time. Diran Alexanian's treatise provides an excellent explanation of the mechanics of the bowstroke,[1] and études such as Popper's Cello Étude no. 27 from the *High School of Cello Playing* will also help. It goes without saying that daily fundamentals practice should always include preparatory études from Feuillard, Popper, Piatti, and so on, but the Elgar *can* furnish material for self-composed études in learning to play uncontrolled spiccato in conjunction with fast runs: that is, a study in both-hands playing. If you cultivate the creative habit of inventing your own études based on the troublesome sections of works in the cello repertoire, particularly the great concertos of the eighteenth and nineteenth centuries, you can isolate problem spots and master their demands. Including repertoire-based études in daily practice makes it easier to maintain a high level

of playing so that you're always ready to give a concert—or take an audition.

The études in this chapter are examples of how to practice skills cellists commonly find most difficult: fast runs, high passages, intonation in double-stops and chords, large and awkward shifts, and others. They demonstrate that reducing a problem to its basic components, or turning it upside down, can solve it.

FAST, REPETITIVE BROKEN CHORDAL PASSAGES WITH STRING CROSSINGS

The cadenza from the Saint-Saëns Cello Concerto no. 1 in A Minor, op. 33, is not particularly hard to start, but as the arpeggiated figure travels downwards, it becomes harder and harder to keep it perfectly in tune (fig. 7.1).

Repeated slow practice of the excerpt will not help very much, except in the earliest stages of note-learning, because the required bowstroke—an uncontrolled spiccato—isn't possible at a slow tempo.

One way to practice this is to turn it into a double-stopping exercise so you can more clearly hear the intervals (fig. 7.2). Start under tempo, listening carefully, but work it up to tempo as soon as possible using the "two steps forward, one step back" metronome technique from chapter 5.

The advantage of this exercise is that it's easier to hear harmonic intonation when the notes are played simultaneously, and therefore we can make adjustments to the third of the triad (which, since all the triads in this passage are in first inversion, is the lowest note of each figuration).

One of the hardest aspects of this passage is keeping the intonation clean in the last three or four chords where the position of the hand is at its widest (fig. 7.3). So why not play the exercise in reversed order so that you start with the more difficult chords? (By the same reasoning,

Figure 7.1. Camille Saint-Saëns, Cello Concerto no. 1 in A Minor, op. 33, movt. II, m. 90

Figure 7.2. Étude after Saint-Saëns in double-stops

Figure 7.3. Étude after Saint-Saëns in reverse motion

it is also a good idea to practice scales and scales in double-stops, starting at the top so that you play the most difficult-to-tune notes while your attention span is at its freshest and most focused.)

A similarly difficult passage in Variation VII of Tchaikovsky's *Variations on a Rococo Theme* can also benefit from the "upside-down" treatment, so that the passage in figure 7.4 becomes the passage in figure 7.5. The broken thirds can similarly benefit from double-stopped treatment for easier hearing of the harmonic intonation, as shown in figure 7.6.

One of the most notoriously difficult broken chordal string-crossing passages in the cello literature comes from the first movement of the Dvořák Cello Concerto (fig. 7.7). Rather than moving sequentially, as in the Saint-Saëns and Tchaikovsky examples, its patterns are more irregular and involve awkward shifts, and its bowstroke is a kind of ricochet that may not come easily at first (a useful preparatory exercise could be applying the bowstroke to an étude such as Piatti's Caprice no. 7 where the left-hand patterns are significantly easier).

The chromaticism of the chords in this passage, as opposed to the relatively uncomplicated triadic formations of the chords in the Saint-Saëns and Tchaikovsky examples, is what makes them so hard to tune. The first step should be to tune the top notes of each chord (see fig. 7.8). Next, continuing to use double-stopped bowing, play the complete chord (see fig. 7.9).

Vary your practice by playing these exercises with different rhythms and tempi. Once you can play the complete chords reliably in tune at your goal tempo, all that remains is to add the ricochet bowings, whose difficulty will be greatly lessened by having perfectly secure intonation. The strength of the left hand reinforces the strength of the right.

DOUBLE-STOPPED PASSAGEWORK

Sixths

These passages are relatives of the previous kind. Harmonic intonation is required, but the chromaticism of the chords often makes it difficult to tune in the heat of the moment.

In this example from the first movement of the Saint-Saëns Cello Concerto, the perfect fifths are difficult to tune (fig. 7.10). This is because the hand must constantly change its angle to make the transition between the fifths and sixths.

This passage can benefit from the same treatment as the Dvořák example above, that is, splitting up the upper and lower double-stops to work on intonation. This

way, we can work first of all on getting the perfect fifths absolutely clean but also on the harmonic intonation of the minor and major sixths. The left and right hands must work together to make a strong tone and clear attacks on the chords, because intonation is affected by dynamics and attack (see fig. 7.11). To vary the repetitions, we can also practice it as an exercise in string crossings instead of double-stops (see fig. 7.12).

Octaves

Some octave passages are relatively uncomplicated in that they are largely stepwise, such as this passage from the third movement of Schumann's Cello Concerto in A Minor, op. 129. The principal difficulty in this example is keeping the tone bright and projecting high on the D- and G-strings (see fig. 7.13). Sometimes, an octave passage has the added complication of a large leap, as in this passage from the third movement of the Saint-Saëns Cello Concerto (see fig. 7.14).

Learning to tune octaves is a matter of hearing both voices. Separating the voices can train the ear and the muscle memory simultaneously to find the correct pitch more automatically, with the caveat that you must keep your hand in the same position you would use for playing both voices simultaneously. Because the lower voice can be the hardest to hear—the ear is naturally drawn to the higher pitch—work on it first to learn the skill of quickly isolating and fixing lower-pitch intonation. Pay especial attention to the measure with the leap from A to F-sharp, taking care to prepare your arm in advance of the shift. Also take care to differentiate between the minor and major seconds in the descending section: the first half of the measure is a chromatic scale, but the second is the bottom half of an A minor scale and contains two intervals of a major second. Tune the C-natural in the fourth measure of the excerpt according to the principles of linear intonation, that is, slightly flat (see fig. 7.15).

Next, isolate the upper voice, also listening closely for intervallic relationships in the linear intonation (see fig. 7.16). An even more simplified approach may be used in octaves passages that contain several sizeable leaps, such as this one from Tchaikovsky's Rococo Variations (see fig. 7.17).

Practice the separate voices with slurred bowings in the manner of an infinity symbol shifting exercise, that is, preparing each shift with a pulling-back motion (see fig. 7.18). The rapid speed of this section means that all joints must be extremely relaxed, because a tense arm cannot shift quickly. Play with a resonant *fortissimo*, because the power of the right arm's weight in the string will influence the efficiency of the left arm's shifts (see fig. 7.19). Because of the difficulty of tuning the leaps,

Figure 7.4. Pyotr Ilich Tchaikovsky, *Variations on a Rococo Theme* op. 33, var. VII, mm. 24–28

Figure 7.5. Étude after Tchaikovsky in reverse motion

Figure 7.6. Étude after Tchaikovsky in double-stops

Figure 7.7. Antonín Dvořák, Cello Concerto in B Minor, op. 104, movt. I, mm. 158–65

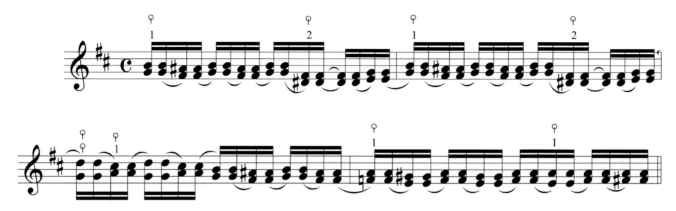

Figure 7.8. Étude after Dvořák in double-stops

Figure 7.9. Étude after Dvořák in double-stops and string crossings

Figure 7.10. Camille Saint-Saëns, Cello Concerto no. 1 in A Minor, op. 33, movt. I, mm. 99–102

Figure 7.11. Étude after Saint-Saëns in lower and upper voices

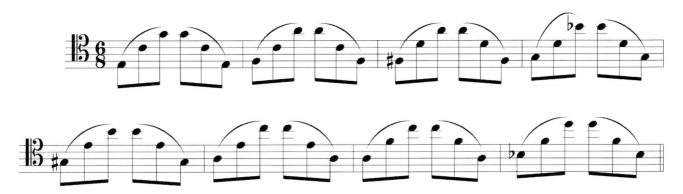

Figure 7.12. Étude after Saint-Saëns in string crossings

Figure 7.13. Robert Schumann, Cello Concerto in A Minor, op. 129, movt. III, mm. 456–60

Figure 7.14. Camille Saint-Saëns, Cello Concerto no. 1 in A Minor, op. 33, movt. III, mm. 65–69

Figure 7.15. Étude after Saint-Saëns in lower voices

Figure 7.16. Étude after Saint-Saëns in upper voices

Figure 7.17. Pyotr Ilich Tchaikovsky, *Variations on a Rococo Theme* op. 33, var. VII, mm. 63–65

Figure 7.18. Étude after Tchaikovsky in lower voices

Figure 7.19. Étude after Tchaikovsky in upper voices

start this exercise at a moderately slow tempo, working it up to the speed of the original using the "two steps forward, one step back" metronome method. As always, maintain the double-stop hand position even when only one voice is played. Sometimes, an octaves passage is complicated with embellishments, as in this notoriously difficult example from the first movement of Dvořák's Cello Concerto (see fig. 7.20).

There is no hope of getting the triplet figures in tune if the basic octaves are not in tune, so the first step should be practicing the octaves using suggestions from above: using the linear concept of intonation, separating the voices, starting at the bottom and working upwards, utilizing the infinity symbol shifting movements, and so on. The next step is getting familiar with putting down the first finger while the thumb and third finger are play-

Figure 7.20.   Antonín Dvořák, Cello Concerto in B Minor, op. 104, movt. I, mm. 327–28

ing an octave. It is more difficult to tune a half-step than a whole-step. You can cultivate this skill by playing a modal scalar étude like the one in figure 7.21.

Don't make the mistake of practicing this exercise with a halfhearted tone "for tuning," because the dynamics and attacks with which you play affect your intonation. All practice for this example should be at a healthy *forte* that really gets the strings vibrating. If it transpires that this is too loud in the context of the piece, you can easily turn the volume down later. Feel the heaviness of your arm's weight in the string, and the gravitational power of the relaxed right arm will help the left arm's shifts go smoothly.

THREE- AND FOUR-NOTE CHORDS

The principles of tuning double-stops apply to three- and four-note chords—that is, harmonic intonation and a strong sense of arm weight and clean bow attack into the string.

There are many ways to play three- and four-note chords, from the "two-and-two" approach to one that is more "rolled." Almost all chords should "break" as early in the down-bow as possible, ideally lower than the balance point. The bow should touch down on the string as close as possible to the frog, and the speed of the stroke should also be slow so that the break occurs in the strong lower half of the bow.

The fundamentals of playing this type of chord can be found in exercise 36 of Louis Feuillard's *Daily Exercises*. This should be a preliminary to any self-composed chords étude.

In Classical- and Romantic-era cello concertos and sonatas, the melodic line is usually found in the top note

of the chord. Breaking the chord in the middle or upper part of the bow therefore weakens the melodic impact of the chord. In these examples from the Elgar and Dvořák cello concertos and Haydn's Cello Concerto in C Major, Hob. VIIb:1, the chords should break in the lower part of the bow (figs. 7.22–24).

The exercise in breaking chords, shown in figure 7.25, strongly requires practicing the chords with a looping stroke that makes the two lower notes speak clearly but that arrives on the top notes no higher than the lower-middle part of the bow. Also practice the chords making all three notes sound simultaneously (or as close to simultaneously as you can) to further reinforce close-to-frog playing. The left hand must inspire and reinforce the right hand's power by engaging the fleshy parts of the fingers with the strings, feeling strong contact around the sides of the string and on the fingerboard. The sensitive use of vibrato will add to the resonance of the chords, provided it doesn't disrupt the intonation. Avoid the temptation to lift the fingers off the string too soon, that is, before the chord has had a chance to resonate well.

PASSAGES WITH AWKWARD SHIFTS

The following examples are characterized by difficult shifts at a high tessitura and a fast tempo. In the second phrase of the first movement of Schumann's Cello Concerto, the intrepid soloist must successfully perform an ascending two-octave arpeggio very quickly—twice (fig. 7.26). Many cellists consider Schumann's Cello Concerto the most difficult to start of all the major cello concertos, for this reason.

The best way to execute such a large shift rapidly is to use the most economical movement possible. Therefore,

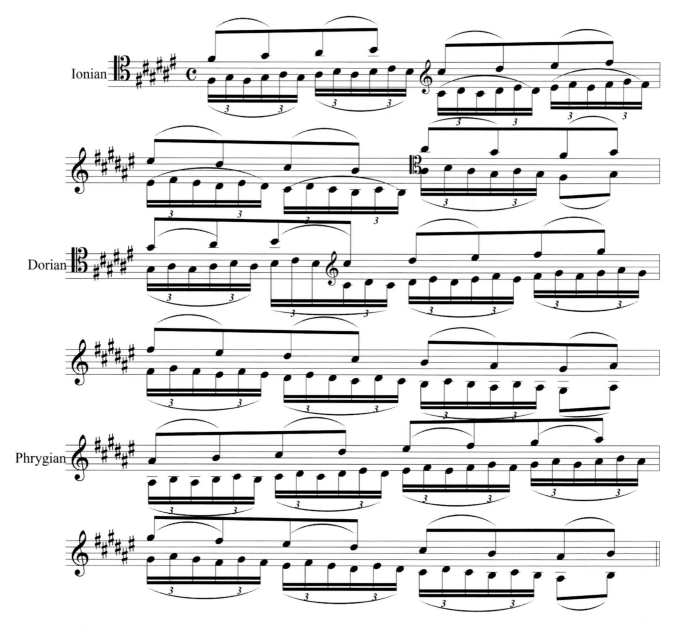

Figure 7.21. Étude after Dvořák in modal scales

Figure 7.22. Edward Elgar, Cello Concerto in E Minor, op. 85, movt. I, mm. 1–2

Figure 7.23. Antonín Dvořák, Cello Concerto in B Minor, op. 104, movt. I, mm. 89–91

Figure 7.24. Franz Joseph Haydn, Cello Concerto in C Major, Hob. VIIb:1, movt. I, mm. 22–24

Figure 7.25. Étude after Dvořák in breaking chords

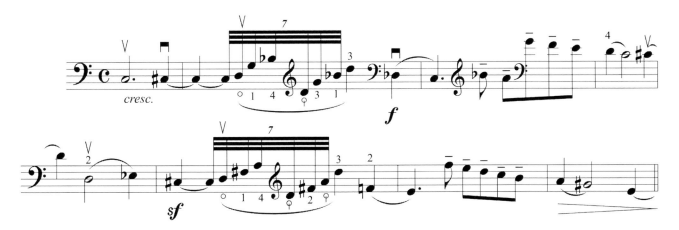

Figure 7.26. Robert Schumann, Cello Concerto in A Minor, op. 129, movt. I, mm. 13–20

have the left arm at the same elevation in first position as you need in thumb position, because the last thing you need is to be flapping your arm about, à la the Chicken Dance.

Having planned the trajectory of the left arm, you can now build up the septuplet, note by note, adding an extra note each time and practicing stopping on it to check for correct intonation and efficient shifting (see fig. 7.27). It is very important to practice the notes of the septuplet at concert speed, because the movement you would use to play this section slowly is different from that needed at tempo. Repeat each section, but not in a hit-or-miss manner. Figure out exactly what conditions must be in place—arm elevation, hand angle, and so on—for the passage to be successful. Then repeat the process and the result until success is much more familiar than failure. With enough perfect repetitions, the transition from neck position to thumb position will become seamless so that you can reliably hit every note of the septuplet in time and in tune.

A similarly difficult passage in the fourth movement of Elgar's Cello Concerto requires a series of leaps of a tritone, embellished with thirty-second notes (see fig. 7.28). Many cellists find this passage difficult to tune. The first step should be to break it down into just the shifts (see fig. 7.29).

Next, taking care to play the thirty-second notes in tempo (the metronome marking for this section is 72 to the quarter note), play the shifts with the embellishments, separating them with an eighth note "stay" between them (see fig. 7.30). Maintain a powerful *fortissimo*, aggres-sively accenting the attack of each new bow. The power of the bowing will help to propel the shifts quickly and accurately up the string.

Similar exercises can be invented for this passage in Variation V of Tchaikovsky's *Rococo Variations* (see fig. 7.31). Practice the shifts in isolation, practice in tempo with "stays" in between shifts, in ascending and descending motion, and so on (see fig. 7.32). Sometimes, rapid sequential shifting passages require smooth, fast shifting in both directions, as in the passage from the third movement of Haydn's Cello Concerto in D Major, Hob. VIIb:2, shown in figure 7.33.

Most cellists keep the thumb resting on the harmonics of the A- and D-strings throughout this passage rather than shifting the whole hand up and down at high speed. Intonation is the most difficult aspect of this passage, and the hardest notes to tune are the D, F-sharp, and C-sharp, which are the fourth, fifth, and sixth notes of the first measure. This is because the shifts are unusual: we don't often have to stretch a perfect fourth between thumb and first finger, for example, nor do we normally need to jump an octave and a half rapidly over two strings using the same finger. Exercises like the following, played in tempo, can help to familiarize them (fig. 7.34).

FAST RUNS WITH SEPARATE AND SLURRED BOWING

One of the hardest types of passagework to play under the influence of performance nerves is a dashing run at

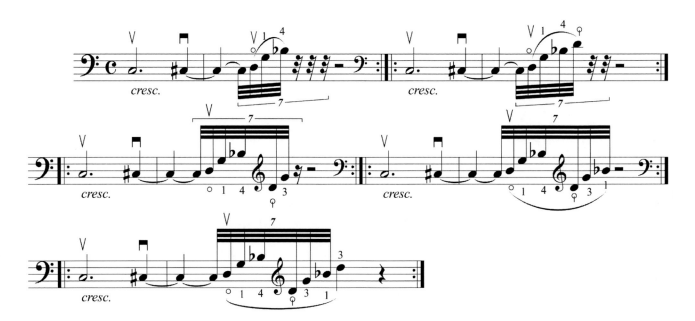

Figure 7.27.   Étude after Schumann using a note-by-note technique

Figure 7.28.　Edward Elgar, Cello Concerto in E Minor, op. 85, movt. IV, mm. 18–19

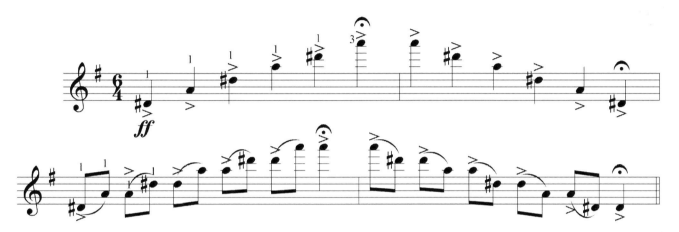

Figure 7.29.　Étude after Elgar in isolated shifts

Figure 7.30.　Étude after Elgar in shifts plus embellishments

Figure 7.31.　Pyotr Ilich Tchaikovsky, *Variations on a Rococo Theme* op. 33, var. V, mm. 9–10

Figure 7.32. Étude after Tchaikovsky in isolated shifts, then shifts plus embellishments

Figure 7.33. Franz Joseph Haydn, Cello Concerto in D Major, Hob. VIIb:2, movt. III, mm. 54–55

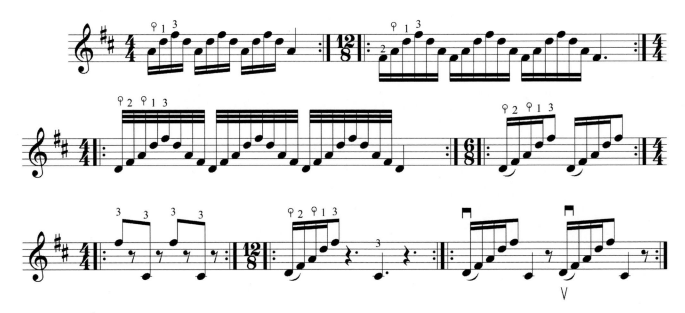

Figure 7.34. Étude after Haydn in arpeggios

a fast tempo. The left hand sometimes becomes so tense, cold, and/or sweaty that the fingers become clumsy and miss notes—and in some extreme cases, the left hand falls off the fingerboard altogether. Part of this problem is related to a lack of mindful breathing and the resulting tension; the breathing and applied kinesiology exercises from chapter 2 will alleviate some of this. Another part of the problem is homolateral use of the arms, where mutual reinforcement of the fingering and bowing is neglected because of exclusive focus on one arm or the other. More than any other type of difficult passagework, it is imperative to play the runs in the following examples up to tempo to train the fingers and bow in the type of integrated movements that are needed in performance.

Sometimes the run takes place on just one string, as in this example from the second movement of Elgar's Cello Concerto (fig. 7.35). In this case, an arm elevation that works for both neck and higher positions, combined with as economical a shifting movement as possible, is key.

Another difficulty in this passage is maintaining a consistent bowstroke, which in this case should be a light spiccato (fig. 7.36). Some players initially find it difficult to coordinate the stroke with the dashing runs. In this case, double the notes while maintaining the same tempo, so that at least you're practicing the stroke up to tempo even if the left hand isn't there yet.

Sometimes a run takes place over two strings, which adds the complication of string crossings to the difficulty of the bowstroke. In this example from Tchaikovsky's *Pezzo Capriccioso*, keeping the bow on "planes" of the A- and D-strings that are close together will help create a seamless transition between strings (fig. 7.37).

Figure 7.35.   Edward Elgar, Cello Concerto in E Minor, op. 85, movt. II, mm. 29–30

Figure 7.36.   Étude after Elgar in spiccato

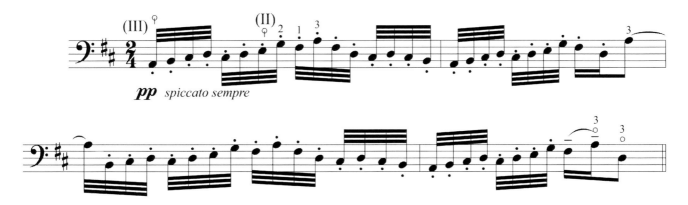

Figure 7.37.   Pyotr Ilich Tchaikovsky, *Pezzo Capriccioso* op. 62, mm. 98–101

Figure 7.38.   Étude after Tchaikovsky in rhythms

The "doubling" exercise used for the Elgar example above can work for improving the spiccato bowstroke. But because it's relatively unusual to play in thumb position low on the strings like this, it's common in the early stages of learning *Pezzo Capriccioso* to stumble over the notes in this passage (fig. 7.38). The first step should be to make sure the base knuckles aren't collapsing: a rounded hand position with gently curved base knuckles is a good starting point for success here. When getting the fingers to move fast enough is challenging, practice rhythmic exercises where some but not all of the note values are augmented. This means you can keep some of the notes at tempo even though some are slowed down.

These rhythmic exercises are also applicable to passages where the fast runs are slurred, such as the one shown in figure 7.39 in the third movement of Saint-Saëns's Cello Concerto, which may be practiced with

the rhythms shown in figure 7.40. Rhythm exercises also help even out "lumps" in slurred runs that contain many string crossings, such as the one in the fourth movement of Elgar's Cello Concerto shown in figure 7.41, which may be practiced as shown in figure 7.42.

SUMMARY OF
COMPOSING YOUR OWN ÉTUDES

The purpose behind making up études is to make difficult passages secure through the isolation and accurate repetition of what makes them difficult. Practice études with expressive commitment and a large, resonant tone in preparation for performing.

The three broad principles in this chapter for composing études are (a) variation of rhythmic and other

Figure 7.39.   Camille Saint-Saëns, Cello Concerto no. 1 in A Minor, op. 33, movt. III, mm. 29–33

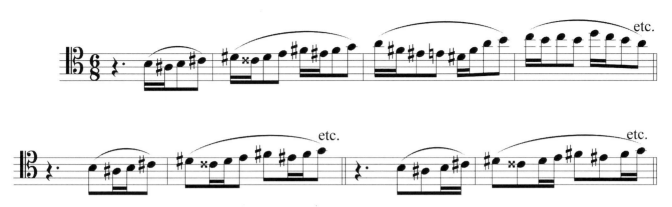

Figure 7.40. Étude after Saint-Saëns in rhythms

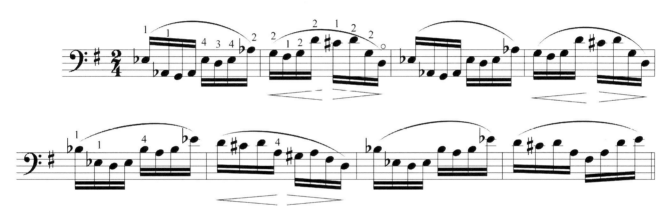

Figure 7.41. Edward Elgar, Cello Concerto in E Minor, op. 85, movt. IV, mm. 84–91

Figure 7.42. Étude after Elgar in rhythms

parameters, (b) reduction, then gradual increase of difficult techniques, and (c) transformation of passages by changing the order of notes.

1. Variation

- Play broken chords as double-stops or chords for familiarization and intonation.

- Play double-stops and chords as broken chords, for the same reasons.
- Practice runs in different rhythms of your own devising so that you can get some of the notes up to speed, even if not all of them are yet.
- In fast passages using separate bowstrokes, try to get the bowstroke up to speed as soon as possible even if the left hand cannot yet play up to speed. You can do this by playing two or four bows to a note.

2. Reduction

- Practice double-stop passages by reducing them to their separate voices. Listen closely for intonation and to figure out exactly where the trouble spots are so you can correct them. Make sure you maintain the correct hand shape for playing both notes, holding both strings down, even though you will only be bowing one of the strings.
- In a passage with a difficult run or awkward shifts, play the passage in tempo but come to a stop on different notes to isolate and fix errors. Start with just a couple of notes, play them perfectly, and then add one more note each time, using as many repetitions as necessary to find a successful method of preparing for and getting through difficulties.

In passages that combine difficult shifts with other challenging techniques, reduce the passage to the shifts alone. Once they are secure, you add the other notes back in.

3. Transformation

- Play a sequential passage backwards to improve fluency.
- When practicing a passage in broken chords, change the order of the notes in which the chord is broken to aid memorization and intonation.
- Practice scalar passages in different modes, or even different keys, to aid intonation, finger flexibility, and intonation.

Chapter Eight

A Practice Session on Fauré's *Élégie*

In this sample practice session, we will apply the techniques outlined in this book to one of the most popular pieces in the repertoire, Gabriel Fauré's *Élégie* op. 24. It's no surprise that Fauré, one of the great masters of French song and an enthusiast of the cello, should have composed such a lyrical piece for the instrument. The *Élégie* provides one of the greatest opportunities in the repertoire for cellists to perform the skill for which the cello is most beloved—a singing, soulful tone.

SCORE STUDY

This score study uses the first printed edition of the *Élégie* by J. Hamelle, Paris, from the 1880s (fig. 8.1). Expressive markings such as articulations and text directions are relatively sparse compared with some modern editions, but this is the version that Fauré himself approved, so it's best to use it as a starting point for an interpretation.

The broad overview of the *Élégie*'s formal plan shown in table 8.1 outlines the five main sections of the piece, appearances of the thematic materials, key structure, tempi, dynamics, and expressive markings. Although it isn't a detailed analysis, it does provide a big picture for future memorization.

Within this five-part structure, four main themes appear. Mark these appearances in the full score and the cello part as a road map for memorization. Sing through all the themes as they appear in the cello and piano parts. Write a list of descriptive words that express the emotion you want to portray in your interpretation, such as those suggested below.

1. First theme (appears a total of four times, always in C minor): "the first time, an anguished cry from the heart; the second time, frightened; the third time, hushed with desolation; the fourth time, furious and impassioned." (See fig. 8.1.)

2. Second theme (countertheme to the first theme; appears only once): "defiant, rebellious." (See fig. 8.2.)
3. Third theme (appears twice; first in A-flat major, later recapitulated in C minor): "the first time, redeeming, soothing; the second time, misty, resigned." (See fig. 8.3.)
4. Fourth theme (appears only once): "an outburst, the dénouement." (See fig. 8.4.)

Take notes in the score as you prepare each theme. Sing through all the themes again, exaggerating the dynamics, articulations, and phrase shapes. Where are the possible high and low points of each phrase? Where are the high and low points of the piece overall?

Other factors to consider include dynamic variation, since Fauré wrote so few instructions for the performer. Another is tempo: Should it be more or less constant throughout, or should the different sections each have their own tempo? How slow can you realistically play the first theme without running out of energy? How fast can you realistically play section C? What is a stylistically appropriate use of shifts and vibrato? There are no right or wrong answers, but it's important to ask yourself these questions so that you can plan a well-thought-out interpretation, rather than one that haphazardly "just happens."

Now it's time to study and compare some recordings. There are dozens of available recordings of the *Élégie*, and the six compared here reflect a wide range of styles and eras of cello playing. That of André Navarra and Annie d'Arco[1] may have some extra historical importance. One of Navarra's few teachers was Jules Loeb, the dedicatee of the *Élégie* and, with the composer at the piano, its first performer. Whether or not Navarra's two-degree separation from the composer makes his recording a primary or secondary document for performance practice is debatable, considering he made it fifty years after his studies with Loeb, but it's still interesting to observe its place in the performance history of the composition.

Table 8.1.   A Brief Formal, Thematic, and Harmonic Analysis of Fauré's *Élégie*

Section	Thematic material and key	Dynamics and markings
A: mm. 1–22	m. 1: Molto adagio. One-measure piano introduction, C minor. mm. 2–5: first theme; cello has melodic voice; repetitive eighth-note chordal accompaniment; begins and ends in C minor. mm. 6–9: second iteration of first theme; similar chordal accompaniment but piano bassline is at a lower octave; begins and ends in C minor. mm. 10–17: second theme (a countertheme to the first theme rather than a developed theme in its own right); briefly tonicizes A-flat in m. 13; ends on dominant of C minor. Interestingly, this second theme never appears again. mm. 18–22: third iteration of first theme; begins in C minor, ends with a repeated deceptive cadence (chords: G to A-flat major).	***mf***, diminuendo ***f*** throughout ***pp***, full score is marked *dolcissimo*, though this doesn't appear in the cello part ***p***, crescendo to arrive at ***f*** in m. 12; m. 14: diminuendo to ***p***; m. 16: molto crescendo to ***ff***, diminuendo ***pp*** throughout
B: mm. 23–34	mm. 23–29: third theme; piano has melodic voice, cello accompanies with motive derived from a four-note segment of the first theme. The second theme is characterized by much shorter note values than the first, and syncopated rhythms in the melodic voice. Begins in A-flat major: Fauré uses the A-flat chord from the deceptive cadence at 21–22 as a pivot to the new key. mm. 30–34: third theme continued; cello takes over melodic voice, piano takes over accompanying motive previously seen in the cello part. A-flat major at the beginning; briefly tonicizes F minor at m. 34; passes through F-sharp diminished seventh chord to get to G chord (dominant of the home key of C minor) at 35.	***pp*** throughout. Sempre molto adagio (both parts), cantabile espressivo (piano part only). m. 28: dolce (piano part only) a tempo, espressivo, ***pp***. mm. 32–33: poco a poco crescendo to an arrival at ***f*** in m. 34
C: mm. 35–38	mm. 35–38: fourth theme; cello and piano alternating virtuoso "outbursts" in fast sextuplets. The piano bassline is derived from the same motive of the first theme that has featured in other "accompaniment" parts. Begins in the dominant of C minor, works its way to a cadence in C minor at m. 39.	***ff*** throughout. Poco ritardando in the second half of m. 38
A': mm. 39–46	First theme; cello has melodic voice; piano accompaniment carries over the fast sextuplet motion from section C. C minor; deceptive cadences at mm. 42–43; cadences into C major mm. 44–45.	a tempo, ***ff***; mm. 43: diminuendo; m. 44: ***p***; mm. 45–46: ***pp***
B': mm. 47–53	Third theme recapitulated; piano has melodic voice mm. 45–46; cello takes over melodic voice mm. 47–53.	m. 47: ***pp*** with crescendo–diminuendo; m. 49: sempre diminuendo; m. 50–53: ***pp***

Figure 8.1.   Gabriel Fauré, *Élégie* op. 24, mm. 1–4

Figure 8.2.   Gabriel Fauré, *Élégie* op. 24, mm. 10–13

Figure 8.3.   Gabriel Fauré, *Élégie* op. 24, mm. 30–31

Figure 8.4.   Gabriel Fauré, *Élégie* op. 24, mm. 35–37

The other recordings compared in the table below include the perennially popular one by Jacqueline du Pré with Gerald Moore[2] from the 1960s, and two from the 1990s by Steven Isserlis with Pascal Devoyon[3] and by Pieter Wispelwey with Paolo Giacometti,[4] and two from the twenty-first century, those of Ophélie Gaillard with Bruno Fontaine[5] and Gautier Capuçon with Michel Dalberto.[6]

To compare every subjective aspect of these interpretations of the *Élégie* would take many pages. However, tempo is one aspect that responds well to a comparative study of these recordings. Table 8.2 shows the metronome markings, measured in eighth notes, during the structural and thematic sections of the *Élégie*. "A:1" denotes section A, first theme; because the first theme is repeated at the end of section A, there is another column for it here, since in some of the recordings it appears in a significantly different tempo from that of the opening measures. The piano and cello versions of the melodic material of the third theme sometimes vary greatly in tempo, so they each have their own column.

We can see from this comparison that most of the cellists, Gaillard aside, take around 6 minutes and 45 seconds to play the *Élégie*. What they do within the time frame is, of course, varied. Pieter Wispelwey keeps the most consistent tempi throughout, speeding up only for sections C and A'. This gives his interpretation a sense of flowing lyrically between sections. Jacqueline du Pré, by contrast, has a very free concept of tempi, which on paper may look a little erratic, but it sounds intensely emotional and highly effective in performance.

Another interesting factor is that in spite of Fauré's tempo marking of *molto adagio*, none of the performers takes an extremely slow tempo. There are good reasons for this: the relatively slow harmonic rhythm in the first theme makes it hard to sustain the listener's interest if the performer takes it any slower than the upper 50s or low 60s, and furthermore, when the first theme comes back in a *fortissimo* dynamic and an octave higher in the A' section, a very slow tempo would be difficult to sustain. It's surely no accident that all six of the performers take this section at a faster tempo than they began the piece.

Table 8.2.   Tempi in Various Recordings of Fauré's *Élégie*

	A:1	A:2	A:1	B:3 piano entry	B:3 cello entry	C:4	A':1	B':3	Overall length
Navarra, 1977–81	Steady, 71	Very steady, 78	71–73	53–58, rubato	57–60	87	72–74	56–60	6:38
du Pré, 1969	63	85	72	60	54, rubato	92	74	68	6:43
Isserlis, 1993	60–63	61–67	60–63	63–66	63–66	70–73	70	56–60	6:58
Wispelwey, 1998	62–63	66–67	63	64–66	62	77, accel.	70	57–60	6:59
Gaillard, 2008	60–64	68	66	60	50, rubato	88, rubato	72, ritard.	52	7:25
Capuçon, 2011	58–64	66–74	60–70	66, rubato	63–67, accel.	89	76	52–55	6:43

Molto adagio ♩ = 15

Use the full compass of the bow; breathe through your bow strokes and vibrato.

Figure 8.5.   Louis Feuillard, *Daily Exercises* **no. 32, mm. 1–11**

Again, there is no right and wrong here, just evidence of a performance tradition that we may wish to consider in forming an interpretation.

PREPARING TO PLAY
FAURÉ'S *ÉLÉGIE* AT THE CELLO

Among the many challenges of this surprisingly difficult piece are the cultivation of a strong, consistently pulled tone in sections A and B and building rapidity in shifting and finger dexterity in section C. Nervous performers sometimes experience a shaking or stiff right arm in the opening measures, and this prevents the tone from having the heart-rending, moving quality the phrase demands. Section C is often out of tune and scrambling, and by the time the player reaches section A', he or she has run out of energy and the tone sounds weak and anticlimactic.

When preparing to play the *Élégie*, your fundamentals practice should preemptively address these issues using études, both precomposed and self-composed. Play the first few variations of exercise 32 from Louis Feuillard's *Daily Exercises*,[7] focusing on the fundamentals of pulling the bow resonantly. Breathe through the stroke, using the "looping" bow changes of the infinity bows exercise from chapter 2 to give your legato a sense of constant motion. Vibrate continuously, because the *Élégie* is the kind of piece where this is appropriate. If self-recordings reveal that you have a habit of unthinkingly stopping

your vibrato, practice the walking fingers exercise from chapter 4 as you practice Feuillard. Consider your fingers as agents of pitch change but your whole arm as an agent of vibrato that doesn't stop just because the fingers have changed the pitches. (The tempo marking and text in fig. 8.5 are mine.)

Of course, a metronome marking of 15 to the quarter note is about twice as slow as the goal tempo of the *Élégie*. Practicing tone with a slower bow speed than you actually need will make the procedure far easier when you have to use it in repertoire—it's the other side of the "two steps forward, one step back" exercise from chapter 5. This exercise works both ways and helps in preparing very and very fast tempi. Transfer this concept of tone into the opening measures of the *Élégie*. Initially, use this *Élégie*-based exercise for practicing the walking fingers exercise and looping bow changes over the string crossings, using the fingering of your choice (see fig. 8.6).

Now it's time to address the question of fingering. Any experimentation with this should include the topic of shifts of expression. It may not be fashionable in the present day to slide audibly as often as performers on historical recordings of the late nineteenth and early twentieth centuries, but most would agree that a limited number of audible slides of expression is appropriate for a Romantic composition. The example below shows some of the possible places for shifts of expression, but obviously you should choose just one or two, not all (fig. 8.7).

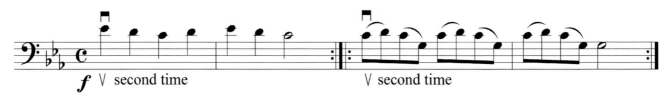

f V second time   V second time

Figure 8.6.   Étude after Fauré in bow changes and string crossings

Figure 8.7.   Gabriel Fauré, *Élégie* op. 24, mm. 1–4, possible shifts of expression

You should plan contrasting fingerings, shifts, and tone colors for the second and third iterations of the first theme. Many performers will play at least one of these starting on the D-string, and this will affect the placement of expressive shifts. If the shift occurs in the same place every time the theme occurs, it becomes predictable, if not cringe-making, to the audience. Starting on the D-string provides at least one more expressive shifting opportunity (see fig. 8.8).

This isn't the last we see of the first theme—it comes back an octave higher at the end of the piece. By this point, an energetic performer may be getting tired. It's therefore important to practice this iteration of the theme using techniques from chapter 4 to cultivate strength and richness of tone without forcing or losing power. Since the string is shortened by having fingers down in the higher register, it's possible—and necessary—to bow extremely close to the bridge without losing the core of the fundamental notes. The arm's weight should be directed heavily into the string using the lower half of the bow, and it will probably not be necessary to use an especially fast bowstroke. The vibrato needs some drama, whether that's from speed or amplitude or both, and it must be consistent. Practice the walking fingers exercise in this high position too, taking care to maintain the curve of the knuckles and to keep the thumb alongside the hand (see fig. 8.9).

The other main section of the *Élégie* requiring extra preparatory attention is, of course, the fast and furious fourth theme, which appears exclusively in section C. Less advanced players often find this challenging, though it needn't be if you ensure the shifts work efficiently. A good preparation for this is Feuillard's exercise 16,[8]

which focuses on shifting to and from the sixth position. Ensure that your arm relaxes at the split second before the shift and that your fingers retain their natural spacing and looseness as you do so, referring to the infinity shifts exercise from chapter 2.

After polishing this technique, turn to the problem at hand—the awkward passage between measures 35 and 36—and reduce it to its bare components by working on the shift separately from the rapid sextuplets (fig. 8.10). Don't forget to bow confidently—successful shifting is a both-hands technique. Inhale and exhale deeply before playing, and breathe consciously through all of the shifts and bowstrokes. Play in a variety of different tempi with a metronome, using the "two steps forward, one step back" procedure until you can play it confidently and accurately with the metronome at your goal tempo. Once you can do this up to speed, you've accomplished the most difficult thing about this passage.

Now add in some, but not all, of the embellishing notes, using the same metronome procedure. This brings the fast turns up to speed, but it allows a little time between each of them as an intermediary step towards playing the complete passage. Continue to bow confidently and breathe deeply while affirming to yourself that your relaxed, efficient bowstrokes are helping your left hand shift accurately and easily and vice versa (fig. 8.11).

When you approach measures 35–36 after having practiced these preparatory exercises, the hurdle of combining fast shifts with quick turns becomes much more manageable. Again, use the metronome at varied speeds, and continue to focus on shifting quickly, accurately, and with relaxation in both arms.

Figure 8.8.   Gabriel Fauré, *Élégie* op. 24, mm. 6–9, possible shifts of expression

Figure 8.9.   Gabriel Fauré, *Élégie* op. 24, mm. 39–42

Figure 8.10.   Étude after Fauré in shifts

Figure 8.11.   Étude after Fauré in shifts plus embellishments

MEMORIZATION

By this point in the learning process, most cellists will have easily memorized parts of the *Élégie* as a by-product of study, listening, and repetition. All that remains is to work on phrases and smaller sections of the piece, and to join them together to form a cohesive, thoughtfully paced interpretation. One of the most important parts of performing from memory is being able to concentrate on the maps and signposts in the music, in both cello and piano parts.

Notice, to begin with, the importance of the number three in the *Élégie*. The first three themes all have the "once, twice, third time goes somewhere different" shape of Classical sentence structure (fig. 8.12). Notice, too, that in each of the three presentations, the piano accompaniment is subtly different. Be able to sing the bassline of each, changing the octave if necessary, at the same time as playing the cello part. This will make rehearsing

it as chamber music easier and contribute to memorizing how the phrases flow into each other.

Unlike the first theme, which ends with a perfect authentic cadence in the home key of C minor on its first two presentations, the second theme is more harmonically adventurous (fig. 8.13). Its first sentence includes a brief tonicization of A-flat major—foreshadowing the modulation to A-flat in section B?—but its second travels back to C minor, reinforcing this with a repeated progression through the German augmented sixth chord to the dominant of C. This added harmonic color gives the second theme a sense of rebellion against the first theme.

When it comes to the third theme, the cello and piano experience a reversal of their previous roles, since the piano is now the one to introduce the melodic material. The cello's sympathetic accompaniment is actually a motive from the second half of the first measure of the first theme, bringing a sense of unbroken connection between themes.

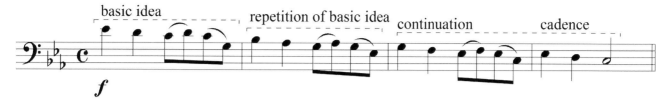

Figure 8.12.   Gabriel Fauré, *Élégie* op. 24, mm. 1–4, sentence structure

Observe how Fauré seamlessly pivots between C minor and A-flat major by way of a deceptive cadence that becomes the new tonic (fig. 8.14). Note the new key area in your score, and memorize the fact that this is the only serious modulation in the *Élégie*, though there are a few tonicizations (brief cadences onto chords other than the tonic). Also notice the way Fauré hands this motive between piano and cello in measure 23; try to imitate the pianist's tone, articulation, and phrasing as you take it over.

As you practice the bassline accompaniment, sing the piano's melody, phrasing your accompaniment to be as sensitive as possible to the harmonic colors. Memorize both lines and the progression of their underlying chords.

When the cello part takes over the melody, it's all too tempting to take off at an entirely different tempo and style—we cellists love a poignant melody. Even though a vibrato and some slides of expression—techniques the piano cannot use—are acceptable as the theme blossoms, try to make the cello's entry as fluid as the continuous rippling line of the piano's middle voice.

This interior passagework for the piano is also part of what gives the third theme rhythmic interest. Notice how the note values Fauré uses—particularly in the piano part—get shorter and shorter the closer we get to the dénouement. From the stately quarter notes and eighth notes of the opening, we work our way up to sextuplets in thirty-second notes in the C and A′ sections. Even if we

decide not to change the tempo dramatically between sections, the faster note values of the accompaniment give a sense of more and more urgent rhythmic drive.

The third theme marks the beginning of this awakening as the syncopations seem to press the dramatic action forward (fig. 8.15). Many performers, in an attempt to sound expressive, put rubato on the triplets by elongating the first one so that it becomes closer to a sixteenth note and two thirty-seconds. This is, I think, a misstep, because one of the most rhythmically interesting things about the third theme is the three-against-four conflict of the melody against the interior passagework.

The next time we see this theme, it's recapitulated into the home key of C minor. The rhythmic shape of the final presentation is unchanged, but the shape of the melodic line is partly inverted. Fauré shapes the harmony as a conflict between the previous, hopeful key of A-flat major and the inevitable pull towards C minor. Listen for, and enjoy, the conflict between the ghost of A-flat major and the relentless C pedal in the piano bassline (fig. 8.16).

As you continue the process of exploration and memorization, look and listen everywhere for the two unifying features of the *Élégie*: the importance of the number three and the cyclical connection of motives from the first theme in all parts of the piece. These structural points will sustain your concentration and memory in performance when muscle memory and chronological memory will not.

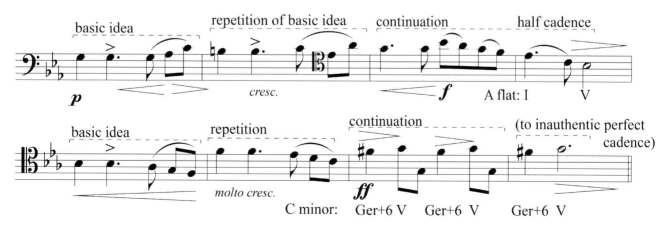

Figure 8.13.   Gabriel Fauré, *Élégie* op. 24, mm. 10–17, sentence structure

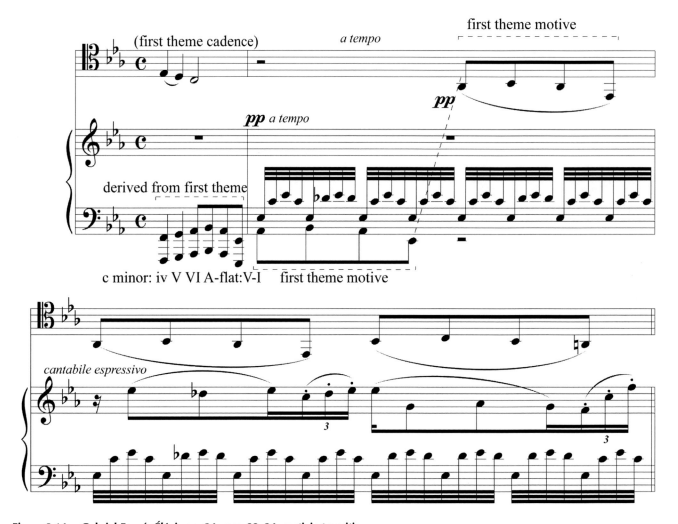

Figure 8.14.   Gabriel Fauré, *Élégie* op. 24, mm. 22–24, motivic transition

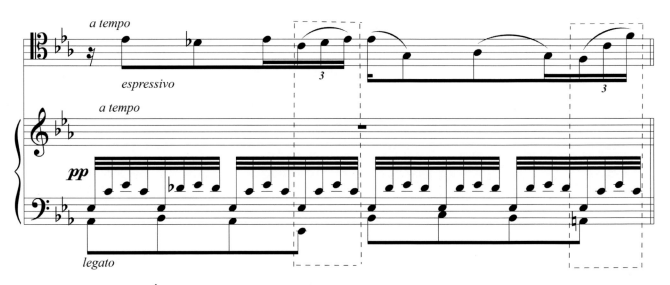

Figure 8.15.   Gabriel Fauré, *Élégie* op. 24, mm. 30-31, cross-rhythms

Figure 8.16. Gabriel Fauré, *Élégie* op. 24, m. 47, tonic pedal

Conclusion

Teacher, Teach Thyself

A DIFFERENT VIEW

In the 1989 film *Dead Poets Society*, a charismatic English teacher played by Robin Williams commands a classroom of privileged but unimaginative schoolboys to climb on their desks to get a different view of the world, and of the poetry they're trying clumsily to analyze.

Playing the cello isn't all that different from studying poetry. It's so easy to get locked into quotidian habits that we get stuck making the same uncomprehending mistakes again and again, or we simply have no idea of how to move forward. Sometimes we need to do something far outside our day-to-day experience to understand what's going wrong.

When I read *A Soprano on Her Head*, Eloise Ristad's classic motivational work for musicians, I was very taken with the central story of a struggling singer who found the tone quality that had previously eluded her by singing on her knees with her head upside down on the floor.[1] It made me wonder if there might be some equivalent for the cello that could be accomplished without having to wear a seatbelt, take out an enormous cello insurance policy, or be an advanced practitioner of yoga.

That was when it occurred to me that cellists could probably approximate a playing position lying on the floor. After some experimentation, I found that I could do this, and the view it gave me of the world was very different indeed.

I lifted the bow to the strings, and started to make my normal preplaying motions. I've always played most solo concerts from memory, but as a somewhat introverted person, I feel shy about looking at the audience, and at that time I often performed with my eyes closed or downcast. Lying on my back on the floor, I unthinkingly looked down.

Except that I didn't. To look "down" at my cello and bow, I had to lift my head *up* off the floor, straining my neck uncomfortably. I had to laugh at myself a little

for that—so ingrained was this habit that I was subconsciously willing to do something mildly painful in order to accommodate it. Teacher, teach thyself!

The next thing that happened was a much pleasanter kind of surprise, and all my students who tried this exercise found exactly the same thing: when you play the cello lying on the floor, you can make an astonishingly big, resonant, free tone. The most common response, after the initial gasp of surprise, is "I didn't know my cello could make so much sound!"

But the sound was within the cello—and within us—all along. All it took to release it was letting go of a few neurotic habits.

Here's what I think happened. When you play lying on the floor, all previous, inefficient habits—bowing primarily in the weaker upper half while neglecting the heavy frog, withholding the weight of the right arm so that the bow only plays on the "surface" of the string, raising your shoulders in an illogical attempt to make a more powerful tone—are instantly gone, because it's uncomfortable to do them in a supine position. When you play on your back, gravity does a huge part of the sound production for you. Playing in the upper half of the bow feels less comfortable than playing at the frog, so you end up making the lower half your default setting for bowing.

Playing on your back isn't exclusively about gravity, but about letting go, both physically and psychologically. You can release everything you were holding up, because the floor is holding you up. It was always there to support you, of course, but you didn't notice because you were too busy with the juggling act of trying to play well and distracted by the ceaseless mental chatter—"Am I in tune? Is my arm moving the right way? Am I going to make the shift?"—that goes with it. This exercise is another of the "reset buttons" for efficient technique that I have discovered in my teaching and playing career. Its effectiveness is no accident. Lying on the floor is a feature in many therapeutic practices, including Alexander

Technique, Feldenkrais, and some forms of meditation, and in all cases it provides a different view, a way to say, "Stop, listen, think."

When taking a different view forces you to let go of inefficiencies, extraordinary things can happen. Even when you return to an upright position, you can remember what "floor tone" sounded like, adopt it as a goal sound, and try to replicate it in the practice room by using the torso-driven, both-handed strategies set forth in this book.

AN UNLIKELY PRACTICE TOOL

What happens, though, when you have to perform? Under the hot lights of the concert stage, it's pretty hard to conjure up that feeling of lying on your back, laughing at yourself. Even after what I'd learned about my habit of looking down while playing, it was incredibly hard to stop doing this. My natural shyness made me incredibly reluctant to look at the audience while I played, for fear of accidentally making eye contact and breaking my concentration. A few years spent playing in a full-time string quartet allowed me to put this problem temporarily to one side, because we always played with the music in front of us, and we had no time to worry about the gaze of the audience because we were looking at our scores, or, more often, at each other.

After I left my quartet and started playing solo recitals and concertos again, I was forced to rethink my habit. During the summer of 2011, while pregnant, I worked on what I called my "Bach 36 Project," in which I made a video blog post of all thirty-six movements of Bach's six cello suites (BWV 1007–1012), one a day for thirty-six consecutive days. I intended it as a gift for the little daughter growing inside me, as a sort of snapshot in time of how I played Bach right then, off the cuff, in my studio with a cheap Flip video camera. Over the course of the thirty-six days, my baby bump got noticeably bigger under the cello, which meant that I had to teach myself a different way to hold the instrument. I expected that my Bach interpretation would grow and develop as the baby did, especially considering that each of the cello suites is progressively more difficult than the preceding one.

What I didn't realize was how the project would cause me to rethink my playing. Of course, I'd seen videos of myself playing in concerts. Like everyone else, I cringed when I watched myself on camera, embarrassed at my mistakes, my facial expressions, and my inefficient movements. I put a lot of this down to the stress of performing and resolved to do better. But when I watched my first Bach videos, which I'd filmed alone in the familiar, stress-free atmosphere of my office, I realized

that my bad concert-hall habits were nothing more than a continuation of the bad habits I was practicing every day. I deleted my first attempt at the Prelude from Cello Suite no. 1 in G Major, BWV 1007, because I couldn't see my face in it—I was so hunched over the cello that only the top of my head was visible in the picture. All my energy was going inwards, and none of my planned expressions made it to my "audience."

I turned off the video camera and spent a couple of hours practicing the Prelude, scales, and études, with my head up. I even wrote "LOOK UP!" on a piece of paper and placed it on the floor in front of me, in case I looked down out of habit and forgetfulness. Then I took a second video of the Prelude, determined to send my energy outwards instead of inwards.

I watched take two, expecting a vast improvement. Yes, it was more accurate and more interesting to listen to. But the picture was almost as disturbing as the one featuring the top of my head. I thought I'd adopted a new, confident stance, but instead I was staring wildly around the room, seemingly unable to focus my gaze on any object for more than a second. I looked hyperactive and scattered, and my playing sounded that way too.

In my next practice session, I decided to fix my eyes on a picture on the wall, a pleasant screen-print of autumn leaves. The resulting video seemed more focused both in appearance and sound, but still my unflinching, straight-ahead stare was a little alarming to look at.

This was certainly an improvement, but being able to look at a picture still didn't solve the problem of not being able to look at the audience. For further evidence of my problem, I took a video of myself delivering a lecture—an activity I enjoy—in the string methods class I taught. I was shocked to see that I looked all around the room while talking, too, with the same wild-eyed expression I'd used when playing the cello in that second Bach video. I couldn't seem to center my gaze, or, apparently, focus my message as I flitted from topic to topic, going off on endless tangents and unnecessary explanations. My audience looked confused. My art, it seemed, was imitating my life.

Just as I seek sound models when I'm learning new scores, I started looking for a role model to help me center my stance in the concert hall and, indeed, the classroom. That's when I thought of television newsreaders.

Turn on a television newscast, and you'll see what I mean. A carefully groomed, conservatively dressed man or woman reads out information while appearing to look straight at us. The newsreader's delivery will be clear and direct, but not a monotone—the rise and fall of the phrases will have nuance, expressive pauses, and clear cadences. His or her stance and gestures aren't rigid and inflexible, but they aren't distracting either.

It takes a lot of training to be a newsreader: usually, a degree in journalism and communications, with some voice training, and an ability to look and dress the part. In fact, it's not unlike the training of a musician. Newsreaders, like musicians, are actors in their own drama, with its conventions, rituals, costumes, and audience expectations.

I wanted to learn how to center myself the way top newsreaders do, so I started doing the unthinkable—practicing in front of the television. This was almost sacrilegious for me, since I'd written vehemently against it in the past.[2] What changed my mind was the number of top musicians I respected who swore by practicing with the television on, including my husband, who keeps a large flat-screen television in his trumpet studio. There is also some scientific evidence that people who live with attention deficit disorder—as I do—can focus better on their work in a high-energy, fast-paced environment, where the brain stem is stimulated to produce norepinephrine. According to Mona Lisa Schulz, we can simulate such an environment by working with the television on.[3]

I kept the set muted, because I wanted to listen closely to my own sound. I started with some slow scales, listening intently as always to my tone, intonation, and vibrato. My goal was to keep eye contact with the newsreader as she addressed me. I didn't know what she was saying, but I imagined we were having an intense conversation in which I talked through my cello. Every so often, the picture would cut to news footage, usually of some bad news, such as a disaster or a war zone. When this happened, I continued to watch the screen, trying to express in sound the sadness and shock such tragedy provoked in me. Then the program would cut back to the newsroom, and my conversation with the newsreader continued.

The problem with watching newscasts is that the news is inevitably sad or alarming, even with the sound off, and I didn't want that to be all I looked at while I practiced the cello. So I switched to nature shows, such as *BBC Planet Earth*,[4] where the stunningly beautiful shots of animals and scenery kept my gaze and attention focused, and it didn't matter that I couldn't hear the narra-

tion. In fact, I ended up using the music I was practicing as a kind of soundtrack—footage of a mother and baby whale accompanied a stately Bach Sarabande, while the comical waddling of a flock of penguins seemed to dance along with a Gigue.

After a while, it became habitual for me to perform as though I wanted to converse with the audience or convey a beautiful landscape or a tragic story. I wasn't afraid to glance into their faces, because I had looked into the faces of newsreaders every day in the practice room. The videos I made of myself during this time, both in concerts and in the practice room, show me looking alert and communicative instead of introverted, dreamy, and unfocused. As if by magic, my movements were more efficient also—I wasn't even having to remind myself to pull the bow using my back, or prepare my shifts. By bringing myself out of hiding behind the cello, I inadvertently taught myself to project my playing more effectively as a conversationalist and storyteller.

There is no substitute for learning to pull the bow consistently, tune triads, plan phrases, and to perfect difficult passages in music, and any good teacher will address these challenges in the studio. But to achieve a higher level of artistry, cellists must look for creative and personally meaningful ways to bring together all the components that go into the preparation for performance. As I stated at the beginning of this book, technique and art are the same thing. What I hope I have demonstrated is that practice and performance are also the same thing. Left-hand technique and right-hand technique are the same thing. Tone and intonation are the same thing. Musical logic and musical intuition are the same thing.

A great cellist is both a student and a teacher. It is said that Pablo Casals, when asked why he still practiced every day, even in his nineties, replied that he hoped to improve. One of the greatest cellists and pedagogues who ever lived, he was also a lifelong student, constantly learning, constantly teachable. If, like Casals, we are open constantly to the creative possibilities for learning, we can become—almost without realizing it—our own greatest teachers.

Appendix

Nondiatonic Scales and Arpeggios

Since nondiatonic compositions by composers such as Debussy, Ravel, Bartók, Stravinsky, Shostakovich, Prokofiev, and their contemporaries are now part of the canon of standard repertoire, it is essential to practice the scales that form much of their musical languages. These scales include pentatonic, hexatonic, and octatonic scales, and their related arpeggios. The fingerings for these scales suggested below are some of many possibilities. Experimentation and internalization are the keys to mastering them.

THE ANHEMITONIC PENTATONIC SCALE

A pentatonic scale is any scale of five notes. Pentatonicism is found in folk music from Asia to Scotland to Appalachia, not to mention in Debussy's Cello Sonata and the string quartets of Debussy and Ravel. The most common pentatonic scale in classical music is the anhemitonic pentatonic scale—one with no half-steps (fig. A.1). Since it's so well-known,[1] it's not usually difficult to translate into scale practice. The notes are a partial collection from the Ionian (major) scale, so it is relatively easy to play in tune because of its familiarity. A drone set to *do* will help in the initial stages of learning.

The whole-tone (hexatonic) scale, composed exclusively of whole-steps, is characteristic of Debussy, Ravel, and their contemporaries. Because there are no perfect fourths or fifths between any of the tones in the scale, there can no dominant harmony. This gives the whole-tone scale the sense of weightlessness and airy pastel colors associated with Impressionistic music and painting.

Two kinds of whole-tone scales are shown in figures A.2 and A.3; between their two collections of pitch classes, they go through all twelve tones of the chromatic scale.

How to practice whole-tone scales

In the first stages of learning the whole-tone scale, students often find it difficult to hear the notes "in their mind's ear." Most end up fishing for notes and playing out of tune, usually sharp. Practicing with a drone is one way to use relative pitch to learn the scale. Another way is to divide the scale into smaller sections. Although the whole-tone scale is not diatonic, it's still possible to use aspects of moveable-*do* solfège to build familiarity with whole-tone language (fig. A.4).

In example (a), the whole-tone scale is divided into three *do–re–mi* patterns, pausing on *mi*. Use this pause to "pivot" and make the former *mi* the new *do*, and make a new *do–re–mi* pattern. Do this once more until you've reached the top of the scale.

Example (b) takes away the pivot note and simply divides the six notes of the whole-tone scale into two sets of *do–re–mi*.

Example (c) teaches larger whole-tone collections by making the scale into two four-note sections of *do–re–mi–fi*. Here, the pivot note is F-sharp, which we respell as G-flat to make it the new *do*.

Sing these exercises in whichever octave works best for your vocal range so that you learn to hear and internalize the pitches, then practice them on the cello. In all cases, use a drone as a reference pitch to build secure intonation, and play with a strong, healthy tone.

THE OCTATONIC SCALE

An octatonic scale is an eight-note scale of alternating whole- and half-steps. Because it outlines the diminished seventh chord—a four-note chord comprising stacked minor thirds—it is known in jazz theory as

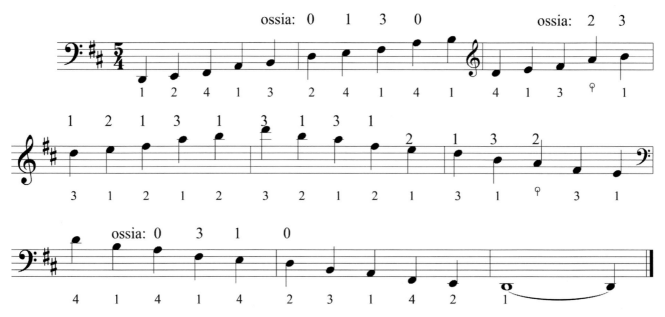

Figure A.1.   The anhemitonic pentatonic scale

the diminished scale. Octatonic collections feature extremely widely in compositions of the late nineteenth and twentieth centuries, so practicing them on the cello can reduce the difficulty of learning pieces such as Kodály's Sonata for Solo Cello op. 8, Bartók's string quartets, and Stravinsky's *Rite of Spring*.

To encompass all twelve tones of the chromatic scale in all possible intervallic combinations, it is necessary to practice three different octatonic scales, shown in figures A.5, A.6, and A.7.

How to practice octatonic scales

The octatonic scale can be even more challenging to internalize than the whole-tone scale. Again, it's much easier to divide it into manageable sections.

Figure A.2.   Whole-tone scale 1

Figure A.3.   Whole-tone scale 2

Octatonic scale 1, for example, becomes much easier if you divide it into three-note sections (fig. A.8). In exercise (a), sing groups of *do–re–me*, using each *me* as a pivot note that becomes the new *do*. Exercise (b) divides the octatonic scale neatly in half, with two sets of *do–re–me–fa* separated by a half-step.

For octatonic scales 2 and 3, it's possible to practice a similar exercise, but with different solfège to reflect that the first two notes are a half-step apart. The syllables *ti–do–re* will work for an exercise in three-note segments, and *ti–do–re–me* for a four-note segment.

Figure A.4.   How to practice whole-tone scales

Figure A.5. Octatonic scale 1

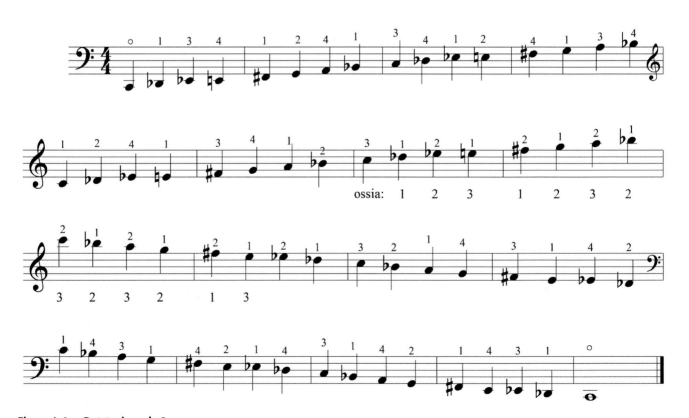

Figure A.6. Octatonic scale 2

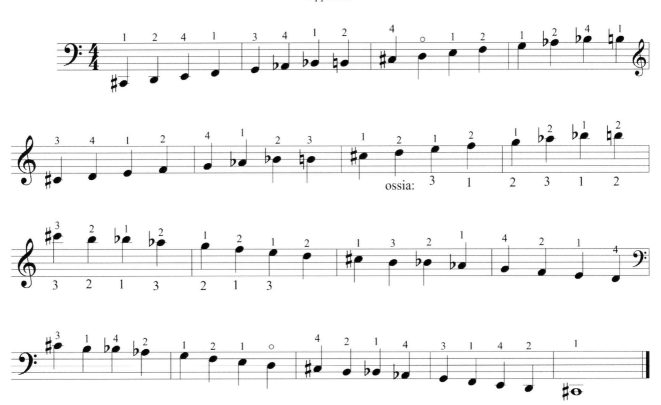

Figure A.7.   Octatonic scale 3

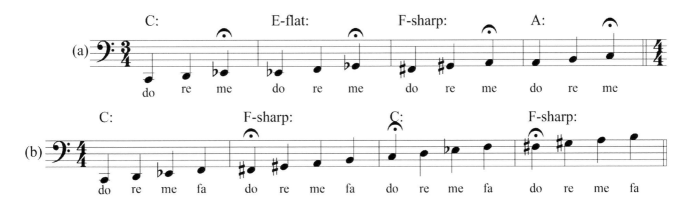

Figure A.8.   How to practice octatonic scales

NONDIATONIC AND UNFAMILIAR ARPEGGIOS

The arpeggio that corresponds to the whole-tone scale is the augmented triad (fig. A.9). Playing it involves mov-ing the left hand in a crab-like motion around the neck of the cello.

The next exercise in arpeggiated seventh chords is not nondiatonic, but part of it may be unfamiliar (fig. A.10). Though it's common to play arpeggios in seventh chords,

Figure A.9.   Arpeggios in augmented triads

the diminished seventh and dominant seventh chords are usually the only ones to appear in most scale books. And yet, it is perfectly common to find a half-diminished seventh or minor-minor seventh chord in the context of a musical composition, where they will appear respectively as chord ii⁰⁷ of a minor key and chord ii⁷ of a major key. The major-major seventh chord is more common in jazz

than in classical music, but we can still find it, in arpeggiated form, as a decorative cadential figure in a few movements of Bach's cello suites.

Practicing these less-familiar scales and arpeggios facilitates learning a large amount of cello, chamber, and orchestral repertoire, and it can also improve theoretical understanding of harmonic and melodic language.

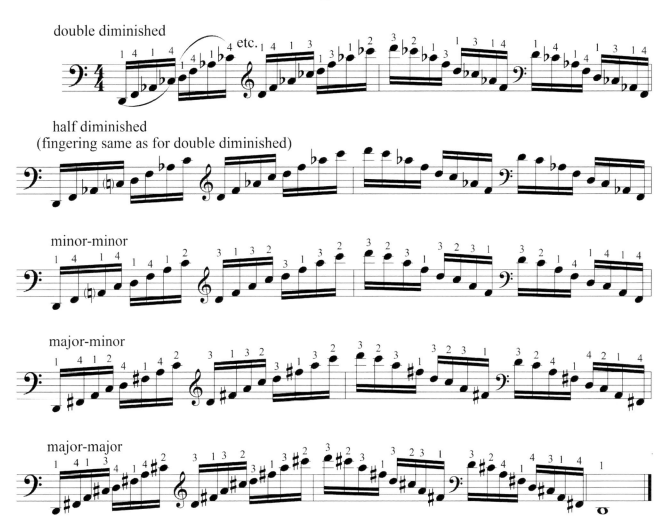

Figure A.10.   **Arpeggios in double-diminished, half-diminished, minor-minor, major-minor, and major-major seventh chords**

Notes

INTRODUCTION

1. For example, Christopher Bunting's *Essay on the Craft of Cello Playing* (Cambridge: Cambridge University Press, 1982) has two volumes, one for the techniques of each hand.

2. Diran Alexanian, *Traité théorique et pratique du Violoncelle* (Paris: A. Zunz Mathot, 1922).

3. Gerhard Mantel, *Cello Technique: Principles and Forms of Movement*, trans. Barbara Haimberger Thiem (Bloomington: Indiana University Press, 1975).

CHAPTER ONE

1. Augustus John, *Madame Suggia*, 1920–3, Tate Britain, London.

2. *Suggia Plays Haydn, Bruch, and Lalo*, with Guilhermina Suggia (cello) and the London Symphony Orchestra, conducted by John Barbirolli, and an unknown orchestra, conducted by Pedro de Freitas Branco, recorded 1927–28, Dutton Labs B0006840H0, 2005, compact disc.

3. Fergus Fleming, *Amaryllis Fleming* (London: Sinclair Stevenson, 1993), 84, 87.

4. "Toyota Unveils Personal-Transport, Violin-Playing Robots," Toyota news release, December 6, 2007. http://www.toyota.co.jp/en/news/07/1206_2.html (accessed September 13, 2014).

5. Donna Eden, *Energy Medicine* (New York: Jeremy P. Tarcher/Penguin, 1998, 2008), 82.

6. K. A. Ericsson, R. Th. Krampe, and C. Tesch-Römer, "The Role of Deliberate Practice in the Acquisition of Expert Performance," *Psychological Review* 100 (1993): 363–406.

7. Nancy K. Napier, "The Myth of Multi-Tasking," *Psychology Today*, May 12, 2014. http://www.psychologytoday.com/blog/creativity-without-borders/201405/the-myth-multitasking (accessed September 13, 2014).

8. Mona Lisa Schulz, *The New Feminine Brain* (New York: Free Press, 2005), 3.

CHAPTER TWO

1. The classic text on dealing with musicians' nerves is Barry Green's *The Inner Game of Music* (Garden City, N.Y.: Doubleday, 1986). See also Eloise Ristad's *A Soprano on Her Head: Right-Side-Up Reflections on Life and Other Performances* (Moab, Utah: Real People, 1982), Kato Havas's *Stage Fright: Its Causes and Cures, with Special Reference to Violin Playing* (London: Bosworth, 1973), and Gerald Klickstein's *The Musician's Way: A Guide to Practice, Performance, and Wellness* (Oxford: Oxford University Press, 2009).

2. The most useful kinesiology book from a musician's perspective is Sharon Promislow's *Making the Brain/Body Connection* (West Vancouver: Kinetic, 1998). Also extremely useful—and fascinating—are Donna Eden's *Energy Medicine: Balancing Your Body's Energies for Optimal Health, Joy, and Vitality* (New York: Jeremy P. Tarcher/Penguin, 1998) and *Energy Medicine for Women: Aligning Your Body's Energies to Boost Your Health and Vitality* (New York: Jeremy P. Tarcher/Penguin, 2008). For an educational perspective, Paul E. Dennison and Gail E. Dennison's *Brain Gym: Teacher's Edition*, rev. ed. (Ventura, Calif.: Hearts at Play, 2010) is exceptionally insightful.

3. Promislow, *Making the Brain/Body Connection*, 120, 133.

4. Also known as the ischial tuberosity, these are the bones we rest our weight upon while sitting.

5. For a comparable description of how this kind of whole-body movement can apply to playing the violin, see Yehudi Menuhin, *Violin: Six Lessons with Yehudi Menuhin* (New York: Viking, 1971), 26–28.

6. Barbara H. Conable and Benjamin J. Conable, *What Every Musician Needs to Know about the Body* (Portland, Ore.: Andover, 1998, 2000), 16.

7. Victor Sazer, *New Directions in Cello Playing* (Calif.: OfNote, 1995), 94.

8. See Gerhard Mantel, *Cello Technique: Principles and Forms of Movement*, trans. Barbara Haimberger Thiem (Bloom-

ington: Indiana University Press, 1975), 56, for a description of the shifting process with reference to physics. See also Sazer, *New Directions in Cello Playing*, 153–54, for a discussion of shift preparation.

9. See Eden, *Energy Medicine*, 74–80.

10. A. Harvey Baker, Patricia Carrington, and Dimitri Putilin, "Theoretical and Methodological Problems in Research on Emotional Freedom Techniques (EFT) and Other Meridian Based Therapies," *Psychology Journal* 6, no. 2 (2009): 34–46.

11. Many musicians use the affirmations in books and audio-books by Louise L. Hay and other motivational authors. See especially Hay, *You Can Heal Your Life*, rev. ed. (Carlsbad, Calif.: Hay House, 2004).

12. See Joseph Sanders and Ruth Phillips, "Freedom to Breathe," *The Strad* 113 (June 2002): 630–34, and Chen Yuan, "Cello Playing and the Chinese Breathing Exercise System, Qi Gong," trans. Yizhou He and Youwen Situ (Beijing, 2001).

13. Sam Pilafian and Patrick Sheridan, *Breathing Gym* (Fort Wayne, Ind.: Focus on Excellence, 2002).

14. There are many variations on deep-breathing exercises that may help to alleviate anxiety and stress, such as the "4-7-8 breath" technique, which is derived from yoga and used by many alternative therapeutic practitioners, such as Andrew Weil. http://www.drweil.com/drw/u/VDR00112/The-4-7-8-Breath-Benefits-and-Demonstration.html (accessed October 15, 2014).

15. For a different version of this exercise, see Menuhin, *Violin*, 17–18.

CHAPTER THREE

1. See Miranda Wilson, "The Principles of String Quartet Intonation," *Strings*, January 2015, 22–25, for a shorter, simplified version of the harmonic intonation guidelines for string quartets detailed in this chapter.

2. See Barry Ross, *A Violinist's Guide for Exquisite Intonation* (Fairfax, Va.: American String Teachers Association, 1989), for a simple, accessible guide to intonation and sympathetic string resonances on the violin. Many of Ross's practical exercises can be adapted for the cello.

3. David Blum, *Casals and the Art of Interpretation* (London: Heinemann Educational, 1977), 102–9.

4. David Doty, *The Just Intonation Primer* (San Francisco: Just Intonation Network, 1993). See also Ross W. Duffin, *How Equal Temperament Ruined Harmony (And Why You Should Care)* (New York: W. W. Norton, 2007).

5. There are many excellent tuner apps for mobile devices, some of which are free. There are also many highly accurate, inexpensive digital tuners.

CHAPTER FOUR

1. For example, Claude Kenneson, *A Cellist's Guide to the New Approach* (Fla.: Exposition, 1974).

2. See also the "serial" exercise on this passage in Janos Starker, *An Organized Method of String Playing: Violoncello Exercises for the Left Hand* (New York: Peer International, 1961), 25.

3. A. W. Benoy and L. Sutton, *Introduction to Thumb Position on the Cello* (Oxford: Oxford University Press, 1969).

4. Rick Mooney, *Thumb Position for Cello* (Miami: Summy-Birchard Music, 1998), *Position Pieces for Cello* (Miami: Summy-Birchard Music, 1997), and *Position Pieces for Cello Book Two* (Miami: Summy-Birchard Music, 2003).

5. Daniel J. Levitin, *This Is Your Brain on Music* (New York: Plume, 2006), 54.

6. Louis Feuillard, *Daily Exercises* (Mainz: B. Schott's Söhne, 1919).

CHAPTER FIVE

1. For an accessible explanation of the science of this process, see Daniel Coyle, *The Talent Code* (New York: Bantam, 2009).

2. Lois Svard, "The Musician's Guide to the Brain," *MTNA e-Journal* (April 2010): 2–11.

3. For further reading on the subject, see Miranda Wilson, "Making the Move from Practice Room to Concert Stage," *Strings*, October 2014, 36–37.

4. See also Miranda Wilson, "Four Post-Tonal Scales for the Cello," *Strings*, August 2014, 24–27.

5. L. Simic, N. Sarabon, and G. Markovich, "Does Pre-Exercise Static Stretching Inhibit Maximal Muscular Performance? A Meta-Analytical Review," *Scandinavian Journal of Medicine & Science in Sports* 23, no. 2 (2013): 131–48.

6. Mona Lisa Schulz, *The New Feminine Brain* (New York: Free Press, 2005), 14–15.

7. Robert Schumann, "Musikalische Haus- und Lebensregeln," *Neue Zeitschrift für Musik* XXXII, no. 36 (1850): 2. In the original German: *Du mußt es so weit bringen, daß du eine Musik auf dem Papier verstehst* (English translation mine).

8. William E. Caplin, *Classical Form: A Theory of Formal Functions for the Instrumental Music of Haydn, Mozart, and Beethoven* (New York: Oxford University Press, 1998).

9. Joseph N. Straus, *Introduction to Post-Tonal Theory* (New Jersey: Prentice Hall, 1990).

10. A full discussion of the philosophy and methods of historically informed performance practice is beyond the scope of this book. For an introduction to this controversial subject, see Colin Lawson and Robin Stowell, *The Historical Performance of Music* (Cambridge: Cambridge University Press, 1999), and Peter Walls, *History, Imagination, and the Performance of Music* (Rochester, N.Y.: Boydell, 2003).

11. Edward Elgar, *Cello Concerto op. 85*, with Beatrice Harrison (cello) and the New Symphony Orchestra, conducted by Edward Elgar, recorded 1928. Digitally remastered in *Elgar Conducts Elgar: The Complete Recordings, 1914–25*, Music & Arts 1257, 2011, compact disc.

12. Ernest Bloch, "Prayer," from *Jewish Life*, with Zara Nelsova (cello) and Ernest Bloch (piano), recorded 1950.

Digitally remastered in *Original Masters: Zara Nelsova*, Decca 000388402, 2005, compact disc.

13. Johann Sebastian Bach, *Cello Suite no. 6 in D Major*, BWV 1012, "Sarabande," with Anner Bylsma (cello), Vivarte 48047, 1993, compact disc.

14. Johann Sebastian Bach, *Cello Suite no. 6 in D Major*, BWV 1012, "Sarabande," with Pierre Fournier (cello), recorded 1961–63. Digitally remastered, Arkiv Produktion 449711, 1997, compact disc.

15. Johann Sebastian Bach, *Cello Suite no. 6 in D Major*, BWV 1012, "Sarabande," with Julius Klengel (cello) and E. Steinberger (piano), recorded 1927. Digitally remastered in *Julius Klengel: A Celebration*, Cello Classics 11024, 2012, compact disc.

16. For an excellent explanation of the benefits of slow practice, see Noa Kageyama, "Is Slow Practice Really Necessary?" http://www.bulletproofmusician.com/is-slow-practice-really-necessary/ (accessed September 24, 2014).

17. Shinichi Suzuki, *Nurtured by Love: The Classic Approach to Talent Education* (Smithtown, N.Y.: Exposition, 1983), 1–3.

18. Christine Carter, "Athletic Advantage," *The Strad* 123, no. 1472 (2012): 42–48.

19. Caplin, *Classical Form*, 35–58.

20. Colin Hampton, *A Cellist's Life* (San Anselmo, Calif.: String Letter, 2000), 25.

21. Mihaly Csikszentmihalyi, *Flow*, rev. ed. (New York: Harper Perennial, 1991), 90–93.

22. For more on this subject, see Louise L. Hay, *You Can Heal Your Life*, rev. ed. (Carlsbad, Calif.: Hay House, 2004), 70–71.

23. Margret Elson, *Passionate Practice* (Oakland, Calif.: Regent, 2002), 86.

CHAPTER SEVEN

1. Diran Alexanian, *Traité théorique et pratique du Violoncelle* (Paris: A. Zunz Mathot, 1922), 203–9.

CHAPTER EIGHT

1. Gabriel Fauré, *Elégie*, André Navarra (cello) and Annie d'Arco (piano), recorded 1977–81, Calliope 9854, 2004, compact disc.

2. Gabriel Fauré, *Elégie*, Jacqueline du Pré (cello) and Gerald Moore (piano), recorded 1969, EMI Classics 91934, 2012, compact disc.

3. Gabriel Fauré, *Elégie*, Steven Isserlis (cello) and Pascal Devoyon (piano), recorded 1993, RCA Victor Red Seal 68049, 1995, compact disc.

4. Gabriel Fauré, *Elégie*, Pieter Wispelwey (cello) and Paolo Giacometti (piano), Channel Classics 10797, 1998, compact disc.

5. Gabriel Fauré, *Elégie*, Ophélie Gaillard (cello) and Bruno Fontaine (piano), Naïve 130, 2008, compact disc.

6. Gabriel Fauré, *Elégie*, Gautier Capuçon (cello) and Michel Dalberto (piano), Virgin Classics 70875, 2011, compact disc.

7. Louis Feuillard, *Daily Exercises* (Mainz: B. Schott's Söhne, 1919), 39.

8. Ibid., 19.

CONCLUSION

1. Eloise Ristad, *A Soprano on Her Head* (Moab, Utah: Real People, 1982), 5–7.

2. Miranda Wilson, "Practice Mythbusters: Common Misconceptions about Practice for Advanced Students," *American Music Teacher* (June/July 2012): 32.

3. Mona Lisa Schulz, *The New Feminine Brain* (New York: Free Press, 2005), 295.

4. *BBC Planet Earth*. http://www.bbc.co.uk/programmes/b006mywy (accessed October 5, 2014).

APPENDIX

1. For a powerful demonstration of the popular accessibility of the anhemitonic pentatonic scale, see Bobby McFerrin, "Notes and Neurons: In Search of a Common Chorus," on *Ted*: "Talks." http://www.ted.com/talks/bobby_mcferrin_hacks_your_brain_with_music (accessed October 14, 2014).

Bibliography

BOOKS AND JOURNALS

Alexanian, Diran. *Traité théorique et pratique du Violoncelle.* Paris: A. Zunz Mathot, 1922.

Baker, A. Harvey, Patricia Carrington, and Dimitri Putilin. "Theoretical and Methodological Problems in Research on Emotional Freedom Technique (EFT) and Other Meridian-Based Therapies." *Psychology Journal* 6, no. 2 (2009): 34–46.

Benoy, A. W., and L. Sutton. *Introduction to Thumb Position on the Cello.* Oxford: Oxford University Press, 1969.

Blum, David. *Casals and the Art of Interpretation.* London: Heinemann, 1977.

Bunting, Christopher. *Essay on the Craft of Cello Playing.* 2 vols. Cambridge: Cambridge University Press, 1982.

Caplin, William E. *Classical Form: A Theory of Formal Functions for the Instrumental Music of Haydn, Mozart, and Beethoven.* New York: Oxford University Press, 1998.

Carter, Christine. "Athletic Advantage." *The Strad* 123, no. 1472 (2012): 42–48.

Conable, Barbara H., and Benjamin J. Conable. *What Every Musician Needs to Know about the Body.* Rev. ed. Portland, Ore.: Andover, 2000.

Coyle, Daniel. *The Talent Code.* New York: Bantam, 2009.

Csikszentmihalyi, Mihaly. *Flow.* Rev. ed. New York: Harper Perennial, 1991.

Dennison, Paul E., and Gail E. Dennison. *Brain Gym: Teacher's Edition.* Rev. ed. Ventura, Calif.: Hearts at Play, 2010.

Doty, David. *The Just Intonation Primer.* San Francisco: Just Intonation Network, 1993.

Duffin, Ross W. *How Equal Temperament Ruined Harmony (And Why You Should Care).* New York: W. W. Norton, 2007.

Eden, Donna. *Energy Medicine: Balancing Your Body's Energies for Optimal Health, Joy, and Vitality.* New York: Jeremy P. Tarcher/Penguin, 1998.

———. *Energy Medicine for Women: Aligning Your Body's Energies to Boost Your Health and Vitality.* New York: Jeremy P. Tarcher/Penguin, 2008.

Elson, Margret. *Passionate Practice.* Oakland, Calif.: Regent, 2002.

Ericsson, K. A., R. Th. Krampe, and C. Tesch-Römer. "The Role of Deliberate Practice in the Acquisition of Expert Performance." *Psychological Review* 100 (1993): 363–406.

Feuillard, Louis. *Daily Exercises.* Mainz: B. Schott's Söhne, 1919.

Fleming, Fergus. *Amaryllis Fleming.* London: Sinclair Stevenson, 1993.

Green, Barry. *The Inner Game of Music.* Garden City, N.Y.: Doubleday, 1986.

Hampton, Colin. *A Cellist's Life.* San Anselmo, Calif.: String Letter, 2000.

Havas, Kató. *Stage Fright: Its Causes and Cures, with Special Reference to Violin Playing.* London: Bosworth, 1973.

Hay, Louise L. *You Can Heal Your Life.* Rev. ed. Carlsbad, Calif.: Hay House, 2004.

Kenneson, Claude. *A Cellist's Guide to the New Approach.* Fla.: Exposition, 1974.

Klickstein, Gerald. *The Musician's Way: A Guide to Practice, Performance, and Wellness.* Oxford: Oxford University Press, 2009.

Lawson, Colin, and Robin Stowell. *The Historical Performance of Music.* Cambridge: Cambridge University Press, 1999.

Levitin, Daniel J. *This Is Your Brain on Music.* New York: Plume, 2006.

Mantel, Gerhard. *Cello Technique: Principles and Forms of Movement.* Translated by Barbara Haimberger Thiem. Bloomington: Indiana University Press, 1975.

Menuhin, Yehudi. *Violin: Six Lessons with Yehudi Menuhin.* New York: Viking, 1971.

Mercier, Anita. *Guilhermina Suggia: Cellist.* Burlington, Vt.: Ashgate, 2008.

Mooney, Rick. *Position Pieces for Cello.* Miami: Summy-Birchard Music, 1997.

———. *Position Pieces for Cello Book Two.* Miami: Summy-Birchard Music, 2003.

———. *Thumb Position for Cello.* Miami: Summy-Birchard Music, 1998.

Pilafian, Sam, and Patrick Sheridan. *Breathing Gym.* Fort Wayne, Ind.: Focus on Excellence, 2002.

Promislow, Sharon. *Making the Brain/Body Connection.* West Vancouver: Kinetic, 1998.

Ristad, Eloise. *A Soprano on Her Head: Right-Side-Up Reflections on Life and Other Performances.* Moab, Utah: Real People, 1982.

Ross, Barry. *A Violinist's Guide for Exquisite Intonation.* Fairfax, Va.: American String Teachers Association, 1989.

Sanders, Joseph, and Ruth Phillips. "Freedom to Breathe." *The Strad* 113 (June 2002): 630–34.

Sazer, Victor. *New Directions in Cello Playing.* Calif.: OfNote, 1995.

Schulz, Mona Lisa. *The New Feminine Brain.* New York: Free Press, 2005.

Schumann, Robert. "Musikalische Haus- und Lebensregeln." *Neue Zeitschrift für Musik* XXXII, no. 36 (1850).

Simic, L., N. Sarabon, and G. Markovich. "Does Pre-Exercise Static Stretching Inhibit Maximal Muscular Performance? A Meta-Analytical Review." *Scandinavian Journal of Medicine & Science in Sports* 23, no. 2 (2013): 131–48.

Starker, Janos. *An Organized Method of String Playing: Violoncello Exercises for the Left Hand.* New York: Peer International, 1961.

Straus, Joseph N. *Introduction to Post-Tonal Theory.* N.J.: Prentice Hall, 1990.

Suzuki, Shinichi. *Nurtured by Love: The Classic Approach to Talent Education.* Smithtown, N.Y.: Exposition, 1983.

Svard, Lois. "The Musician's Guide to the Brain." *MTNA e-Journal* (April 2010): 2–11.

Walls, Peter. *History, Imagination, and the Performance of Music.* Rochester, N.Y.: Boydell, 2003.

Wilson, Miranda. "Four Post-Tonal Scales for the Cello." *Strings*, August 2014, 24–27.

———. "Making the Move from Practice Room to Concert Stage." *Strings*, October 2014, 36–37.

———. "Practice Mythbusters: Common Misconceptions about Practice for Advanced Students." *American Music Teacher* (June/July 2012): 30–32.

———. "The Principles of String Quartet Intonation." *Strings*, January 2015, 22–25.

Yuan, Chen. "Cello Playing and the Chinese Breathing Exercise System, Qi Gong." Translated by Yizhou He and Youwen Situ. Beijing, 2001.

INTERNET RESOURCES

British Broadcasting Corporation. *BBC Planet Earth.* http://www.bbc.co.uk/programmes/b006mywy.

Kageyama, Noa. "Is Slow Practice Really Necessary?" *The Bulletproof Musician* (blog). http://www.bulletproofmusician.com/is-slow-practice-really-necessary/.

McFerrin, Bobby. "Notes and Neurons: In Search of a Common Chorus." On *TED*: "Talks." http://www.ted.com/talks/bobby_mcferrin_hacks_your_brain_with_music.

Napier, Nancy K. "The Myth of Multi-Tasking" (blog post). *Psychology Today*, May 12, 2014, http://www.psychologytoday.com/blog/creativity-without-borders/201405/the-myth-multitasking.

Toyota Motor Corporation. "Toyota Unveils Personal-Transport, Violin-Playing Robots." News release. http://www.toyota.co.jp/en/news/07/1206_2.html.

Weil, Andrew. "The 4-7-8 Breath Technique" (video). http://www.drweil.com/drw/u/VDR00112/The-4-7-8-Breath-Benefits-and-Demonstration.html (accessed October 15, 2014).

RECORDINGS

Bach, Johann Sebastian. *Suites for Unaccompanied Cello*, BWV 1007–1012. Anner Bylsma (cello). Vivarte 48047, 1993, compact disc.

———. *Suites for Unaccompanied Cello*, BWV 1007–1012. Pierre Fournier (cello). Recorded 1961–63. Arkiv Produktion 449711, 1997, compact disc.

———. Julius Klengel (cello) and E. Steinberger (piano). Recorded 1927. *Julius Klengel: A Celebration.* Cello Classics 11024, 2012, compact disc.

Bloch, Ernest. "Prayer," from *Jewish Life*. Zara Nelsova (cello) and Ernest Bloch (piano). Recorded 1950. *Original Masters: Zara Nelsova.* Decca 00388402, 2005, compact disc.

Elgar, Edward. *Cello Concerto op. 85.* New Symphony Orchestra. Sir Edward Elgar, with Beatrice Harrison (cello). Recorded 1928. *Elgar Conducts Elgar: The Complete Recordings, 1914–25.* Music & Arts 1257, 2011, compact disc.

Fauré, Gabriel. *Élégie.* Gautier Capuçon (cello) and Michel Dalberto (piano). Virgin Classics 70875, 2011, compact disc.

———. *Élégie.* Jacqueline du Pré (cello) and Gerald Moore (piano). Recorded 1969. EMI Classics 91934, 2012, compact disc.

———. *Élégie.* Ophélie Gaillard (cello) and Bruno Fontaine (piano). Naïve 130, 2008, compact disc.

———. *Élégie.* Steven Isserlis (cello) and Pascal Devoyon (piano). Recorded 1993. RCA Victor Red Seal 68049, 1995, compact disc.

———. *Élégie.* André Navarra (cello) and Annie d'Arco (piano). Recorded 1977–81. Calliope 9854, 2004, compact disc.

———. *Élégie.* Pieter Wispelwey (cello) and Paolo Giacometti (piano). Channel Classics 10797, 1998, compact disc.

Suggia, Guilhermina. *Suggia Plays Haydn, Bruch, and Lalo.* London Symphony Orchestra, conducted by Sir John Barbirolli. Unknown orchestra, conducted by Pedro de Freitas Branco. Recorded 1927–28. Dutton Labs B0006840H0, 2005, compact disc.

Index

Alexander Technique, 115–16

Alexanian, Diran: *Traité théorique et pratique du Violoncelle*, xv, 87

amateur musicians, 32

analysis: of Bach's Suite No. 4 in E-flat Major, BWV 1010, Bourrée II, 41, *42*; of Fauré's Élégie, op. 24, 106–7, 109–12; harmonic, thematic, and formal, 16–17, 41, 47, 78

anxiety. *See* performance anxiety

arpeggios: in Haydn's Cello Concerto in D Major, Hob. VIIb:2, *100*; of major and minor triads and their inversions, *23*, 40; in Schumann's Cello Concerto in A Minor op. 129, 95, *97*, *98*; of seventh chords and augmented triads, 40, 119, 123–24

attention deficit disorder, 117

Bach, Johann Sebastian: Harpsichord Concerto, BWV 1056, *Arioso*, 28; *O Ewigkeit, du Donnerwort*, BWV 20, "Solang in Gott im Himmel lebt," 22; Orchestral Suite No. 2, BWV 1068, *Air*, 28; Six Suites for Unaccompanied Cello, BWV 1007–1012, 16, 55, 116–7, 123 (Suite No. 1 in G Major, BWV 1007, 72, *74*, 116; Suite No. 2 in D Minor, BWV 1008, 23, *24*, 77; Suite No. 3 in C Major, BWV 1009, 55, *56*; Suite No. 4 in E-flat Major, BWV 1010, 41, *42*, 60, *61*, *62*, 72, 80; Suite No. 5 in C Minor, BWV 1011, 56, *57*; Suite No. 6 in D Major, BWV 1012, 43, *44*, *45*, *59*, 77)

Barber, Samuel: *Adagio for Strings*, 84

Bartók, Béla: Six String Quartets, 40, 119, 120

Benoy, A. W., 30

Beethoven, Ludwig van: Cello Sonata in A Major, op. 69, 19, *20*, *21*, *30*, *31*, *37*; Cello Sonata in G Minor, op. 5, no. 2, 47, *48*; Piano Trio in E-flat Major, op. 1, no. 1, 60; String Quartet in F Major, op. 59, no. 1 ("Razumovsky"), *68*, *69*, *83*; String Quartet in E-flat Major, op. 74, 60–61, *62*, 77, *80*; String Quartet in B-flat Major, op. 130, 83; String Quartet in C-sharp Minor, op. 131, 57, *58*; String Quartet in F Major, op. 135, 57, *58*; Symphony No. 3 in E-flat Major, op. 55, 60

Bloch, Ernest: recording of "Prayer" from *Jewish Life*, 43

Boccherini, Luigi: Cello Concerto in B-flat Major, arrangement by Friedrich Grützmacher, 80; Cello Sonata in A Major, G. 4, 29, *30*

bow: fear of dropping, 4, 8; hold, 3, 27, 29;

bowing: Baroque, 43; Beethoven's markings, 49; breathing with, 3, 12, 13, 109; changes, 8, 9, 28, 33, 37, 108; consistency in, 27, 101, 108, 117; contact point with string, 8, 28, 109; distribution, 45; common errors in technique, 30, 95, 115; expressive choices in markings, xv, 33, 41, 43, 45, 46, 49; at the frog, 32, 95, 109, 115; in fundamentals, 40; in infinity symbol exercises, 8–10, 108; interdependence with left-hand movements, iv, 3–4, 29, 33, 36, 37, 46, 87, 98, 101, 109; shaking, 11; speed, 18, 27–29, 38, 108; stroking initiation from the torso and collarbones in, 9, 117

bowstrokes, 3,8, 28, 36, 39, 87, 89, 101–3, 109

Brahms, Johannes: Cello Sonata in F Major, op. 99, 68; String Quartet No. 1 in C Minor, op. 51, no. 1, 56, *57*; String Quartet No. 2 in A Minor, op. 51, no. 2, 79–80, *81*, *82*; String Quartet No. 3 in B-flat Major, op. 67, 83, *84*

brain-body connection, 4, 7

breathing: alternate nostril exercise, 12; audibility while playing, 11, 13; exercises, 8, 10–13, 39, 41, 128n12, 128n13, 128n14; and performance anxiety, 4, 7; through bowing, 3,12, 109; in phrasing, 43; and tension, 101; through shifts, 12–13, 109; and yoga, xv, 12

Bunting, Christopher: *Essay on the Craft of Cello Playing*, 127n1

Bylsma, Anner, 43–45

Caplin, William: *Classical Form*, 41, 47

Capuçon, Gautier, 107

Carnegie Hall, 51

Carter, Christine, 47

Casals, Pablo, 11, 16, 18, 25, 36, 117

centering exercises, 11

cerebral cortex, 7

conducting, 49

conductors, 27

cross-laterality: exercises, 3, 8, 11, 39, 51; in bowing, 7; in everyday activity and cello practice, 3–4, 39; in infinity symbol exercises, 8–10; march, 8; in shifting, 4, 13; in vibrato, 7

Csikszentmihalyi, Mihaly: *Flow*, 49

About the Author

The New Zealand–born cellist and writer **Miranda Wilson** made her solo debut at the age of sixteen, playing Elgar's Cello Concerto with the Orchestra Wellington. She holds a bachelor's degree from the University of Canterbury in New Zealand, a master's degree from Goldsmiths College, University of London, and a doctorate from the University of Texas at Austin.

Wilson has performed as a soloist, chamber musician, and orchestral player on five continents, and she has made several compact disc and broadcast recordings. She was a founding member of the Tasman String Quartet, an all-New Zealand ensemble, which performed widely on the international concert and competition stage before disbanding in 2009. Since 2010, she has been a professor of cello at the Lionel Hampton School of Music, University of Idaho, where she is also the founder and co-director of the University of Idaho Music Preparatory Division, and co-director of the Idaho Bach Festival. She enjoys writing about music for *Strings* and other publications.

Wilson is married to the American trumpeter Sean Butterfield. They live in northwest Idaho with their daughter. Visit her website at http://www.mirandawilsoncellist.com.